VISIONS BEYOND THE VEIL

VISIONS BEYOND THE VEIL

Visions of Heaven, Angels, Satan, Hell, and the End of the Age

H.A. BAKER

WHITAKER
HOUSE

Publisher's note:
This new edition from Whitaker House has been updated for the
modern reader. Words, expressions, and sentence structure have
been revised for clarity and readability.

Unless otherwise indicated, all Scripture quotations are taken from
the King James Version of the Holy Bible.

VISIONS BEYOND THE VEIL
new edition
(Previously published under the title *Visions of Heaven*)

ISBN-13: 978-0-88368-786-4
ISBN-10: 0-88368-786-0
Printed in the United States of America
© 1973, 2006 by Whitaker House

1030 Hunt Valley Circle
New Kensington, PA 15068
www.whitakerhouse.com

Library of Congress Cataloging-in Publication Data
Baker, H. A.
Visions beyond the veil / H.A. Baker.—New ed., updated & rev.
p.   cm.
Summary: "Chronicles the supernatural visions of the Chinese
orphans at the Adullam Rescue Mission that was founded by
H. A. Baker and his wife"—Provided by publisher.
ISBN-13: 978-0-88368-786-4 (trade pbk. : alk. paper)
ISBN-10: 0-88368-786-0 (trade pbk. : alk. paper)
1. Baptism in the Holy Spirit.   2. Church work with children—
China—Yunnan Sheng.   3. Visions.   I. Title.
BT123.B24 2006
248.2'9—dc22   2005031086

3 4 5 6 7 8 9 10 11 12 **UJ** 15 14 13 12 11 10 09 08

Foreword

Here is an especially revealing book with a window on new worlds—a realm that some have dreamed of, but never knew existed. H. A. Baker lived in this "realm of the Spirit" for more than fifty years after his baptism in the Holy Spirit.

But even before receiving the baptism, the Lord had blessed the Bakers with fruitful labor in the mission fields of Tibet from 1911 to 1919. Many had told them that it was impossible to convert even one Tibetan to Christ. But within a period of six years, they had learned the language and developed a love for the people that was so intense that they had no desire to ever come back to America. The hearts of the Tibetans opened more and more to the gospel, and the prospects for a strong work seemed very promising.

But when his wife, Josephine, took sick, it finally became necessary for them to return to the States. At that time, it seemed as thought they would never again return to the mission field. But God had a purpose in bringing them home; both of them received the baptism in the Holy Spirit.

Shortly thereafter, a letter came from a church offering to give them one thousand dollars in airfare if they would return to the mission field at once.

For a second time they were propelled into missionary orbit, but this time the Lord indicated that they were to go to China, and that they were to be faith missionaries with no denominational sponsorship.

Ministry in China was exiting. In the southwest corner of Yunnan, the most southwest province of China, was a little town of 5,000 called Kotchiu. The Bakers were warned that Kotchiu was overrun by bands of theives. In fact, it was said to be the worst town in all of China. But the Bakers settled there in the midst of vile and sinful surroundings, and began to let the Light of God shine out.

Almost immediately, they were conscious of the many teenage beggar boys who were starving and dying in the streets. That was when they decided to open an orphanage—the Adullam Home. In addition to dysentery and other internal diseases, these boys had terrible sores all over their bodies.

Josephine found great joy and satisfaction in removing their filthy rags and giving them baths. Disheveled hair was cut and clean clothes were distributed. Their sores healed rapidly as they responded to the love of Jesus.

There were forty boys in the Adullam Home when the great miracle took place. In this most unlikely of places, there was an outpouring of the Holy Spirit, the likes of which has seldom been reported in the Christian faith. Uneducated, street orphans fell prostrate on the floor under the power of God. While in the Spirit, they were given visions into the next world. They saw and spoke with angels; they played in the wonderful parks of paradise; they saw the saints of old.

This outpouring went on for many days. These young Chinese children standing and preaching under the anointing of the Holy Spirit, receiving revelations of invisible worlds and the glories of the redeemed.

After the communist takeover of 1949, the Bakers fled to Formosa where he ministered until his death on November 3, 1971. On that morning, Brother Baker strapped on his battery-operated P.A. system, shouldered a bag of tracts, and walked down the lane in Miaoli, spreading the

Good News. He arrived back home before lunch and busied himself typing a letter to a friend in the States. The native cook looked in at the door and called him to eat. She said that he smiled as he answered but seemed in no hurry to arise. When she returned later in the afternoon, she found him slumped over his typewriter unconscious. On Sunday morning around two o'clock, his heart finally stopped beating.

On Thursday, in accordance with his wishes, a very simple funeral service was held outside his home. It was attended by those to whom he had faithfully ministered, as well as a few missionary friends. He is buried beside his wife, Josephine, in LiShan, Miaoli, awaiting the sounding of the last trumpet.

Because I was his editor and publisher, Mr. Baker and I were in constant communication during the last years of his life and ministry. It was through these letters that I learned of his experiences in China.

We rejoice in this newly revised edition of *Visions Beyond the Veil*, published by Whitaker House, and pray that Brother Baker's writings will continue to bless humanity.

—T. A. Lanes

Contents

Introduction 11

1. Mighty Outpouring of the Holy Spirit........... 21

2. Supernatural Manifestations
   of the Holy Spirit... 31

3. Scriptural Results of the Outpouring............. 43

4. Visions of Heaven 61

5. Paradise 79

6. Angels in Our Midst.. 93

7. The Kingdom of the Devil 99

8. The End of This Age and the Return
   of Christ.. 127

9. Chinese Beggar Boy Prophesies.....................145

10. Some Light on Writing the Bible 155

11. The Homeland...165

12. The Way...175

About the Author 187

Introction

The children and young people of the Adullam Rescue Mission were, for the most
part, beggars in the streets of the city. In
some cases they were poor children with one or
both parents dead. Some were prodigals who had
run away from homes in more distant parts of the
adjoining provinces. These children, mostly boys
ranging in ages from six to eighteen, had come to
us without previous training in morals and without education. Begging is a sort of "gang" system
in which stealing is a profitable part. Their moral
code was what would be expected of a gang soci-
ety in a godless land.

The Bible was carefully and daily taught in
the Adullam Home, and the gospel was constantly
preached. Since the children coming into the home
had always been open to the Christian teaching

even before the outpouring of the Holy Spirit, some of them were recent converts, while others had a very good knowledge of the main themes of the Bible.

All of the children who received the Holy Spirit knew enough to believe in one God and to trust in the blood of Christ for salvation. These children truly sought Christ. We did not see anyone who was merely seeking the visions or manifestations that were received day by day. Jesus Christ alone was sought and magnified throughout all the weeks of the Spirit's outpouring.

During this visitation from the Lord, all were treated impartially. The oldest and the youngest, the first arrivals and the latest comers, the best and the worst, all sitting together around their common Father's table, were alike treated to His heavenly bounties.

This falling of the Spirit was clearly a love gift of grace *"apart from works"* or personal merit. It was not something that was worked up; it was something that came down. It was not the result of character building by man from below; it was a blessing of God that came from above.

I am convinced that the experiences of these Adullam children were not manufactured. These wonders simply could not possibly have been the product of the natural minds of these children. Such uneducated, untrained, unimaginative boys as these could not have conceived of such things of their own accord.

Nor could these spiritual experiences, visions, and revelations have been the working of their subconscious minds. These children were too young, too ignorant, or too recently rescued from paganism to have such a thorough handle of biblical teaching on these subjects.

Neither can these things be explained by the psychology of mental suggestion from others. We ourselves had never experienced such visions as were given these children. These experiences were new to all of us. Furthermore, the children did not get these things from one another. When the power of the Lord fell in our midst, many children were filled with the Spirit at the same time. Those who were in different rooms would often receive simultaneous visions of the same things. We looked for this, but there was no opportunity to compare one with another.

The complete harmony of these visions covering countless details is beyond any natural explanation. Even the most ignorant children, who would easily be confused on cross examination, whether questioned singly or in groups, gave clear and uniform answers to questions covering a great number of details.

Nor can these experiences be explained as any sort of mental excitement, religious frenzy, natural emotion, nervous state, nor any sort of self-produced condition. This outpouring of the Holy Spirit came to ordinary children as they went about the not-very-exciting daily routine of going to school.

At first, many of us were quite skeptical as these visions and revelations began to manifest. We approached the subject with many doubts and questions. But we were reminded that supernatural visions and revelations are the foundation upon which the church was established and upon which it stands. In fact, the very Bible itself, Old and New Testament, is a supernatural revelation from God.

In the Old Testament, God often revealed His will to men by speaking through prophets by direct inspiration. God revealed Himself to men in dreams, in visions, and through various kinds of supernatural revelations. Angels brought messages to men and were continually active as God's ambassadors in carrying out His plan of redemption on earth. The Lord appeared to men and spoke to them in a "voice" and with "words." He thus spoke to Moses, as man speaks to man, face to face. (See Exodus 33:11.)

Likewise, much of the New Testament claims to be a supernatural revelation. Paul said of the gospel he preached: *"For I neither received it of man, neither was I taught it, but by the revelation of Jesus Christ"* (Galatians 1:12). What he wrote in all his epistles was simply a part of this supernatural *"revelation of Jesus Christ."*

When Herod wanted to destroy the baby Jesus, the wise men were warned of God in a dream. (See Matthew 2:12.) An angel appeared to Joseph in a dream. (See Matthew 2:13.) A man of Macedonia appeared to Paul in a vision. (See Acts 16:8-10.) At Corinth, the Lord spoke to him in the night by a vision. (See Acts 18:9.) When he was praying in the temple at Jerusalem he fell into a trance and saw Jesus, who spoke to him giving directions for his work. (See Acts 22:17.) Peter also fell into a trance while praying on the housetop. He saw a vision and heard the Lord speaking to him in a voice with words. (See Acts 10:9-15.) An angel appeared to Cornelius in an open vision by day. (See Acts 10:1-3.) The whole book of Revelation was given to John as a supernatural revelation when he was *"in the Spirit."* It is a revelation from the Lord who spoke to him in *"a great voice,"* and it is also a record of visions given in the Spirit and through the ministry of angels. (See Revelation 1:9-11.) Either *"out of the body"* or in vision *"caught up"* to heaven like our Adullam children, Paul was given access to heaven and there saw paradise. He had such an abundance of these supernatural revelations that the Lord had to send him a thorn in the flesh to keep him humble. (See 2 Corinthians 12:1-7.)

> In the early church when God answered prayer, everybody knew He had answered.

Angels had a large part in the work of the first church, also. The early disciples were often protected and directed in their work by the angels. In this way they were delivered from the imminent dangers of earthly powers. An angel spoke to Philip, directing him to Gaza. (See Acts 8:26.) An angel stood by Paul and talked with him, encouraging and directing him. (See Acts 27:23-24.) Cornelius, his household, and his friends were led into the way of salvation and into the baptism of the Holy Spirit through the words of an angel who came to him. This angel, appearing in bright apparel, talked with him, directed him to send for Peter, and then departed. (See Acts 10:1-3.) When Peter was in prison, an angel rescued him. This angel loosened the chains from Peter's hands, told him to get dressed and put on his shoes, opened the prison door and the city gate that was locked, and led Peter into the street. (See Acts 12:7-8.)

Greatest of all the supernatural manifestations in the early church were those of the mighty Holy Spirit, who came to those people just as the Lord had promised He would after He ascended to the Father.

The first Christians did not read prayers. Instead, they prayed to God from the heart, and God directly and supernaturally answered these heart cries. When some of their fellow Christians were in danger, they met together and prayed to God. This was not formal praying; it was not a cringing, heartless, carefully worded prayer meeting for men's ears. Everybody prayed at the same time; everybody cried to God in a loud voice. This was a special prayer meeting for one great need.

When God answered, everybody knew He had answered. The Holy Spirit shook the house in which these people were praying, and everyone was *"filled with the Holy Spirit"* and with mighty, superhuman power. (See Acts 4:31.) Then they boldly went out to spread gospel fire in the very face of death.

The early church experienced the living God. Through the Holy Spirit, they had Jesus in their midst. He worked in them and through them supernaturally by gifts of the Holy Spirit:

> *For to one is given by the Spirit the word of wisdom; to another the word of knowledge...to another faith...to another the gifts of healing... to another the working of miracles; to another prophecy; to another discerning of spirits; to another divers kinds of tongues.*
>
> (1 Corinthians 12:8-10)

I ask you, where is this Living God who brought Israel up out of Egypt with a mighty hand before the eyes of the heathen? Where is our God who once answered in a voice that men could hear, whose voice shook the whole earth? What has become of the God who sent his angels to walk and to talk with His people?

Indeed, what has become of the angels?

And the Christ of the Bible, where is He? Have they taken away our Lord so we cannot find where they have laid him?

What has become of His "Promise"? Jesus said, *"It is expedient for you that I go away: for if I go not away, the Comforter will not come unto you; but if I depart, I will send Him unto you"* (John 16:7). *"He that believeth on me, the works that I do shall he do also"* (John 14:12).

So Jesus has gone back to his Father. But where, oh, where is the Holy Spirit Who was to come to take His place, and to carry on His uncompleted task, to work in the midst of His church in signs and wonders and gifts of the Holy Spirit? Has God died? If so, when? Or has God withdrawn so far away that He cannot hear? Is it impossible for God to talk any more? Have the angels deserted us for some other universe? If so, when did they forsake us? After all, is this Holy Spirit merely a gentle influence? Where is the Holy Spirit Who shook and filled a whole house of praying disciples and through them shook the world?

If ever there was a Living God, if ever there were angels, if ever there was a wonder-working Christ, if ever the Holy Spirit was given, if ever the Bible came as a supernatural revelation from God; then such trances, visions, revelations, and workings of the Holy Spirit as were given to our Adullam children are supernatural visitations from God such as we should expect.

These trances, visions, revelations, and super-natural manifestations were often experienced by the supernaturally founded, supernaturally filled, and supernaturally directed church of the New Testament—the only church the Bible tells or fore-tells anything about.

—H.A. Baker

one

Mighty Outpouring
of the Holy Spirit

Chapter 1

Mighty Outpouring
of the Holy Spirit

The morning prayer meeting was lasting longer than usual. The older children left the room one by one to begin their studies in the school room, while a few of the smaller boys remained on their knees, praying earnestly. The Lord was near. We all felt the presence of the Holy Spirit in our midst. Some who had gone out returned to the room.

Such a mighty conviction of sin—a thing for which we had prayed so long—came to all, so much so that with tears streaming from their eyes and arms up lifted they cried out to the Lord for the forgiveness of their sins, which now seemed so black. One after another went down under the mighty power of the Holy Spirit until more than twenty were prostrated on the floor. Although unsure of what was exactly happening, I was aware that the Lord was doing a most unusual thing in our midst.

I went over to the schoolroom and told the boys that if they felt led to come and pray they might be excused from their lesson. I thought that a few might take the offer. But in a short time, their Chinese teacher was left sitting alone by the table. All his pupils flooded into the prayer room where they were soon praying and whole-heartedly praising the Lord. When the teacher realized there was nothing for him to do, he left to return home. I had not invited him in with the children, for, although he had been with us along time, he seemed utterly dead to any spiritual understanding of the gospel. After going a short distance, the teacher returned.

> I was aware that the Lord was doing a most unusual thing in our midst.

Nobody noticed when he entered the prayer room, for everyone was intent on his own business with the Lord. The teacher went to the farthest corner of the room, where, for the first time in his life, he knelt down and tried to pray. As the

Lord's power was obvious, I felt it best to leave the young man by himself and not to intrude on what I knew could only be the work of the Holy Spirit. It was not long before I noticed the teacher with arms uplifted, tears on his face, pleading with the Lord to forgive his sins, which I heard him say were so very, very many. He was quite a proud young man. For him to humble himself in this way in the presence of his pupils meant a powerful Holy Spirit conviction of sin.

The meeting continued hour after hour; yet the children showed no desire to leave. There was nothing for me to do or say, as the Lord seemed to have complete control. I did my best to stay out of His way.

Something Decidedly New

Eventually an agonized cry went up, beyond anything I had ever heard or imagined, as in visions the children saw the horrors of hell, the anguish of lost souls, and the indescribably evil power of the devil and his angels. Many witnessed themselves bound and dragged to the very brink of hell. Condemnation for sins and the power of the devil over them became a terrifying reality. But freedom from this evil power through the grace of the Lord Jesus was just as real. When they experienced this liberating power from the clutches of the evil one, salvation was made as real as condemnation had been. Great joy, laughter, and peace resulted from the knowledge of what they had been saved from. This was a realization that I am sure they would never be able to forget.

Having been in the very presence of the Lord since the early morning, by the time their late afternoon meal was ready, I thought surely the service for the day was over. Not so. Some left the prayer room for a short time, but all were soon back, saying they wanted to wait upon the Lord all night. This was something decidedly new; previously some had claimed that an hour service was too long. For so long we had wanted them to pray more. Now that it was actually happening, why stop it? Not a child went to sleep until late that night and it was not until six o'clock the next morning that the last stalwarts ended the prayer and praise service that had lasted over twenty hours with scarcely a pause.

After the first two days of this mighty downpour of the Holy Spirit, it seemed to slack off. Thinking that may be all there was, we went back to the regular order of work, expecting to spend more time in the evening, waiting and praying before the Lord. The boys went to their schoolwork, and

I went out to call on some people to talk to them about the gospel.

The morning prayer meeting began at about half past seven. As usual, we all prayed at the same time, and each left when he pleased. Upon returning at noon, I heard someone praying in the prayer room. It was our quietest and most timid boy, Wang Gia Swen, a boy of about eight years of age, hidden behind the organ praying in a loud voice and weeping as he confessed his sins before the Lord. It turned out he had been praying continuously since the morning service without stopping for breakfast.

Great joy and peace resulted from the knowledge of what they had been saved from.

As I came out of the prayer room, the boys were being released from their classes. They were then to go to the garden or to the other kinds of industrial work for the rest of the day, but some of them wanted to know if they could stay and pray. Having been told that those who wished to might remain and pray, a few went to work, but all the others went into the prayer room and began praying. Almost at once there was another mighty outpouring of the Holy Spirit.

This outpouring was so continuous that, for over a week, no more attempts were made to do regular work. We did only the most necessary of things. Everyone spent the rest of the time absorbing the great blessing of God.

In those first days no one paid much attention to eating and sleeping. Whenever the young folks began to pray, the power of God would fall, prostrating many to the floor. It became impossible to have meals at regular hours without interfering with the work of the Holy Spirit. As the power of God would lift from different ones they would go out for a time of rest or to get a snack. When they returned to the prayer rooms, they were soon back under the power of the Holy Spirit again.

> Whenever the young folks began to pray, the power of God would fall.

These manifestations of the Spirit were so continuous that someone was under His power nearly all day long until late into the night. By nine or ten in the evening, when things became quieter, we would suggest that all go to bed and rest until the next morning. Several asked if they could continue to pray and wait upon the Lord. As these few continued in prayer nearly all those who had gone to bed would get back up and return to join them in prayer. Very little sleeping was done during these nights. Some of the boys never left the prayer rooms all night long. When they got sleepy, they rested on the floor for a while and then got up to seek the Lord again. Soon they were lost once more in the things of God.

Staying Out of the Way

One thing was certain. This was a Holy Spirit outpouring that demanded nothing on the part of the "professional" missionaries except to stay out of the way and not interfere with His wonderful work. Our part was to open up our own hearts that we, too, might be taken deeper into the heavenly blessings that were falling in such mighty torrents.

Our presence or absence in these prayer meetings made little difference. On one of those first mornings we were delayed in getting downstairs. Without any call to prayer meeting, one child after another had gone into the prayer rooms where they began to pray and praise the Lord. By the time we finally got down to the prayer rooms we found several of the younger children lying on the floor under the power of the Holy Spirit, singing in other tongues as the spirit gave them utterance.

From the very beginning, the manifestation of the Spirit was moving into the supernatural realm far beyond our own limited knowledge or experience of supernatural matters. Things were happening so fast that my wife, Josephine, and I confessed to each other that our only recourse was to go along with it, fully believing that God was bigger than the devil. We took refuge behind the promise that those who sought the Father for bread would not get a stone (see Matthew 7:9); that those who sought a fish would not get a serpent; that those who sought an egg would not get a scorpion; that those with pure motives like these children, who sought the Holy Spirit, would not get evil things or demons, but would get exactly what they sought: the Holy Spirit. (See Luke 11:13.)

In the following weeks God would prove that promise true. And since He had proved that promise to us before, it set us free from anxiety as we began to witness the wonderful things of God that took place in our midst. Every day was different as one wonder followed another. Day by day, hour-by-hour, our wonder-working God took His Adullam refugees from stage to stage and from glory to glory in His school of the Holy Spirit.

two

Supernatural Manifestations of the Holy Spirit

Chapter 2

Supernatural Manifestations of the Holy Spirit

Many of the most miraculous manifestations of the Holy Spirit fell upon those who knew virtually nothing of what the Bible said about the subject. For us, this was further confirmation of the supernatural nature of these visions and a confirmation of the reality of the outpourings of the Holy Spirit recorded in the New Testament.

The Latter Rain

Some children who had never heard us speak of the present day outpouring of the Holy Spirit as "the latter rain" actually experienced that very thing in this outpouring upon Adullam.

As we all prayed and praised the Lord together with closed eyes, some of the children seemed to feel water dropping on their heads. They were so busy seeking the Lord they did not want to hinder the blessing by opening their eyes to look around. At the same time, in their hearts they wondered how it could be sprinkling rain on them when they were inside with a roof over their heads. But as the sprinkling continued, their hearts were refreshed. As the dropping of water seemed to increase and the sprinkling water became a shower, it all seemed so glorious that the wonder of how it could possibly rain in a downstairs room became irrelevant. The sprinkling became a shower, the shower became a great downpour, and the downpour became a deluge filling the room, rising higher and higher until those children felt submerged in this wonderful, life-giving flood from heaven. At different times, several different children experienced this same sense of the downpouring rain.

Several of the children experienced this same sense of the downpouring rain.

Six months after this great outpouring, after a "dry spell," the floodgates of heaven opened up once again, and we experienced another down-pouring of the Holy Spirit. Again, two of the small children experienced rain, *the latter rain,* which seemed to fall upon their heads, penetrating and flooding their entire being.

> *He hath given you the former rain moderately, and He will cause to come down for you the rain, the former rain, and the latter rain in the first month.* (Joel 2:23)

Through Bible study and through direct revelation by the Holy Spirit, Adullam came to understand the meaning of this *"rain"* as spoken by Joel the prophet. The *"former rain"* was a foretelling of the outpouring of the Holy Spirit upon the first church, sown on the earth on the day of Pentecost and during the succeeding two or three hundred years. (Agriculturally speaking, in Israel, the *former rain* was the rain in the autumn upon the grain that was sown in the ground.) Then came the great *"falling away"* (2 Thessalonians 2:3), the long winter of the dark ages; the grain sown in the earth—the church in the world—was apparently dead.

Then came sprinklings of the *"latter rain"* in the first month of the spring through men such as Luther, Wesley, Fox, Finney, Moody, and other servants of God. Salvation by faith, the *"born again"* experience, and holy living; now, the sprinkling is becoming a shower. Healing through faith in Jesus reappears. The Lord is again casting out devils, healing the sick, raising the dead, proving to be none other than the Almighty God in the midst of those who believe Him. The hope of the Coming King has revived. The Lord is again baptizing believers in the Holy Spirit as in the beginning, *"the former rain,"* so that they speak with other languages and prophesy as the Holy Spirit give utterance. (See Acts 12:4.)

The pouring out of the latter rain is at hand; the clouds are now filling the sky.

The harvest is near. *"The former rain,"* the seed rain, came moderately; *"the latter rain,"* the harvest rain, will come abundantly to ripen the grain, to perfect the church. There will be deluges of rain, the latter rain of the Holy Spirit. The greatest revival the world has ever seen is just ahead. The greatest miracles, the most marvelous wonder-working church the world has ever seen is near. The pouring out of the latter rain is at hand; the clouds are now filling the sky. According to His promise, the Lord will soon pour out his *"Spirit upon all flesh"*

(Joel 2:28). The church that was sown in the time of the *"former rain"* and fell into the earth and died has come forth. Beyond anything that happened right after the days of Pentecost:

> *Your sons and your daughters shall prophesy, your old men shall dream dreams, your young men shall see visions: and also upon the servants and upon the handmaids in those days will I pour out my Spirit.*
>
> (Joel 2:28–29; Acts 2:17–18)

Because of this final, great outpouring of the Holy Spirit, the church in full blossom will have restored to it the years eaten by the locust, the cankerworm, the caterpillar, and the palmer worm. (See Joel 2:25.) The fruits and gifts of the Holy Spirit will all be restored to the true church of blood-washed believers. In its supernatural life and supernatural ministry, multitudes will be converted. *"The floors shall be full of wheat, and the fats shall overflow with wine and oil"* (Joel 2:24); *"a great multitude, which no man could number, of all nations, and kindreds, and people, and tongues"* (Revelation 7:9).

If you read Acts 2, you will see that this outpouring upon *"all flesh"* is for today. Anyone who had been with us at the Adullam Home would be assured of this. Many times the Lord has stood in the midst, made to them the same promises He made to the first believers, and commissioned them with the same commission to carry the same gospel in the same power with which He sent forth the first disciples in the day of the *"former rain."* We know that *"the latter rain"* that fell on Adullam is like the former rain, but it is the last rain that will bring the wheat and tares to full harvest and separation, ushering in the return of the wheat to the barns and the burning of the tares in the furnace fire.

Manifestations of the Holy Spirit

On many different occasions, various Adullam residents perceived the Holy Spirit as a tongue of fire upon the head of each person in the room. In some instances more than one received this vision at the same time. Of course, anyone who is familiar with the Bible knows that the things of God are not equally revealed to all.

When the Spirit had fallen in our meetings many felt the Holy Spirit as a wind blowing upon them, flooding their souls with peace and power. These breezes from heaven were sometimes with such power that we had no difficulty in believing the record that when the first disciples met together and *"they lifted up their voice to God with one accord....the place was shaken where they were assembled together; and they were all filled with the Holy Ghost"* (Acts 4:24, 31).

On several occasions, older and younger children alike saw the Holy Spirit represented as seven lamps. At times of special outpourings of the Holy Spirit, these seven lamps of fire were seen being let down from heaven into the room in our very midst. At other times, in the visions of the throne of Christ in heaven, the children saw the *"seven lamps of fire burning before the throne, which are the seven Spirits of God"* (Revelations 4:5). But we all recognized that the seven lamps meant that the Holy Spirit was in our midst.

> All of us recognized that the seven lamps meant that the Holy Spirit was in our midst.

The Light of Heaven

In the first days of the outpouring of the Spirit, one small boy spoke in pure prophecy when, in the Spirit, he seemed to be in heaven at the very feet of Jesus. The Lord spoke through him in the first person clearing up several things that the children did not understand and telling them how to wait on God and how to seek the Spirit.

Through that small boy, the Lord said:

> When the Spirit is in your midst do not open your eyes, for that will hinder. The Holy Spirit will descend to give you power to preach the gospel, to cast out demons, and to heal the sick. The Holy Spirit is in seven colors—red, blue, and other colors.

One of the older boys then said that when the Spirit had been upon him he had seen a great red light as well as other colors. The word from the Lord explained this to him and to others who had seen different colors. Of course I knew that light is made up of seven colors, but I had never thought of the seven lamps before the throne of God as being the seven colors. Color is light. All light comes from God, and God is light.

These Adullam boys also saw the Holy Spirit, brighter than the noonday sun. This manifestation of the Holy Spirit as a great light became very common. Some children, having opened their eyes to see if it was emanating from an electric light in the room, could scarcely discern the lights in the room because of the exceeding glory of the light of heaven, which seemed to fill the place. These children discovered what Paul meant when he said that on the Damascus road the light that shone about him was *"a light from heaven, above the brightness of the sun"* (Acts 26:13). After their visions of heaven and this great light—brighter and clearer than any they had seen on earth—our Adullam boys knew why in heaven *"there shall be no night there; and they need no candle, neither light of the sun; for the Lord God giveth them light"* (Revelation 22:5). Through these manifestations and revelations, these one-time-beggar children in this dark land on this dark earth knew beyond a doubt that in the New Jerusalem in heaven *"the city had no need of the sun, neither of the moon, to shine in it: for the glory of God did lighten it, and the Lamb is the light thereof"* (Revelation 21:23).

three

Scriptural Results of the Outpouring

Chapter 3

Scriptural Results of the Outpouring

T here are no doubts in my mind that this outpouring of the Holy Spirit was from God. It fulfilled, to exact detail, biblical prophecies foretelling the results that are to follow outpourings of the Holy Spirit.

For instance, one of the results that first manifested among us was a clear assurance of salvation through visions and other workings of the Holy Spirit. The existence of sin and the lost condition of each child was made so real that every bit of hope was forsaken until the Lord, in undeserved mercy, answered the prayers of the lost and saved them. Then the Holy Spirit made the salvation and grace of God just as real and intense as the desolate lost condition had felt. One after another, many of the children went through this process, resulting in a clear experience of salvation. This resulted in the transformation of the life and testimony of the Adullam family, and left no doubt that the home was now made up of many who were born again.

The whole atmosphere of the place changed. The joy, unspeakable and full of glory, came in until it bubbled over. As the boys were at work spading ground for a garden, they praised the Lord so much that other boys in the neighborhood mocked them saying, "Praise the Lord," whenever they met out boys.

> The whole atmosphere changed; the joy, unspeakable and full of glory, came in until it bubbled over.

When one boy went into a store to buy nails, without realizing it, he said, "Hallelujah! I want some nails." This same boy had a wonderful experience from the start. One day on his way to work he danced down the street in the joy of the Holy Spirit, praising the Lord somewhat in the style of Billy Bray, the old Cornish, dancing preacher.

Being cleansed from their sin and born again of the Holy Spirit and still seeking more and more of the Lord, these children were ushered into the deeper things of God until over twenty of the Adullam children spoke in other tongues, as people did on the day of Pentecost; as they did when the Holy Spirit was poured forth at the House of Cornelius; as they did when they received the fullness of the Spirit at Ephesus; as the apostle Paul did; and as the Samaritan Christians undoubtedly did when they received the Holy Spirit in mysterious power and manifestation, so striking and wonderful that Simon wanted to buy it.

Although most of these Adullam boys had never seen such demonstrations, they had been taught to seek the Lord for the Holy Spirit. They were not only rewarded with great *"joy unspeakable and full of glory"* (1 Peter 1:8) in their own hearts, but they received confirmation about their baptism in the Holy Spirit. They knew they received the baptism the same way the New Testament saints did in the beginning, as shown by the five biblical examples just mentioned.

Prophetic Visions

These Chinese boys and girls were saved by the same Lord and baptized in the same Holy

Spirit as the first disciples; for, like them, they not only spoke with other tongues but also prophesied as the Spirit gave them utterance.

No one present at the time has ever doubted that the Lord spoke to us by direct inspiration in those first days when He spoke through one of the smallest and humblest of the children. There was something about the voice and the penetrating power of those words. It was a heart-gripping power that cannot be described. We had never heard such a captivating voice from God in any sermon in all our days. We all knew we were hearing directly from the Lord.

We had never before heard such a captivating voice from God in any sermon.

Quite a number of the Adullam residents later spoke in prophecy. We marveled more and more at the miracles that were taking place as the Lord spoke the wonderful things of God, revealing His plans and purposes by selecting these outcast "nothings" of the earth, recent beggar boys, to become a direct mouthpiece for the living God. We were humbled that God would speak through them by direct inspiration, edifying and building up this little group of simple blood-washed believers so recently saved out of hopeless physical and spiritual despair.

Visions of Things to Come

Another striking result of the work of the Holy Spirit was the way in which He fulfilled the promise that when He, the Comforter, came He would take of the things of Christ to show to His disciples and would show them *"things to come"* (John 16:13). It seemed most wonderful how the Spirit revealed to these relatively uninformed believers the things of Christ, His salvation, and the things of the future through visions of the unseen worlds.

Many of these visions were given to several boys at the same time. Nearly all of the visions were seen by quite a number of people. In many cases the children came to us to ask if the Bible said anything about certain things they had seen in a vision. These visions, witnessed by both younger and older boys, were seen while they were under the power of the Holy Spirit. They were not experienced as a dream but as real life.

Visions of Christ

Some of the visions reflected the details of Holy Week. There was Christ, tied to a post and scourged.

Christ bleeding on the cross as scoffers looked on, His body taken from the cross, carried to the tomb, placed in the tomb, and the tomb closed. There was an angel opening the tomb, Christ's resurrection, His appearance to the women, to the disciples by the sea, and to those in the upper room. Some saw the ascension of Christ and the descent of the two angels.

Almost all saw heaven, detailed visions inside the New Jerusalem in heaven, the angels, and the redeemed. They also saw hell, the misery of the lost, demons, the great tribulation, and the devil himself. Some saw things pertaining to saints and to the subjects of the beast during that time, the battle of Armageddon, the binding and imprisonment of Satan in the pit, the binding of the Anti-Christ, the devil cast out of heaven, the Great Supper of God, and birds eating flesh of kings and captains of the earth.

There were visions of the coming of Christ with his angels, the changing of the sun and moon, "heavenquakes" and earthquakes and destruction that are to attend the coming of Christ and the resurrection of the righteous. Other visions portrayed the Marriage Supper of the Lamb in paradise, as well as detailed views of our mansions and other heavenly scenes.

This magnificent work of the Holy Spirit through visions, as well as in the heart, created such a great interest in further Bible study that even the smaller children wanted to know if they could stop studying "earthly books" so that they could only study the Bible.

Since the unseen world had become so real, it was no wonder that there was a change in our life of prayer and praise. While not all the Adullam residents spoke in other tongues, all except those with mental handicaps were anointed and filled with the Holy Spirit in a much greater measure

No wonder there was such a change in our life of prayer and praise!

than ever before so that Adullam was often lifted up to heavenly places in Christ to joyfully praise and worship the King. Although there were times when one almost began to wonder if these heavenly citizens would come "down to earth" again, there was no need to fear. For it was not long until we saw boy after boy after boy in real intercessory prayer pleading with God for the lost, praying that God would use us all as real warriors for Him in the battle of righteousness. Prayer had become so much more than a mere formality. All now knew that our foes were spiritual hosts of wickedness in heavenly places.

Preaching in the Streets

After two or three weeks of the Lord's dealing with them, nearly all the children, even the younger ones, desired to share the messages they had received. What followed was some real preaching in the power and demonstration of the Holy Spirit. These young boys, both young and old, hardly seemed like our boys when they preached under the real anointing of the Holy Spirit. Despite their lack of knowledge and experience, they didn't speak timidly and apologetically as they had before, but with a sense of great authority. Hell and heaven, the devil and his power, Christ, His blood, and His salvation, were no myths or mere theological concepts to these boys. They knew that the Lord commanded them to preach, and they had been given their message, "Repent, for the Kingdom of heaven is at hand." As we listened to these powerful messages preached with great assurance, warning people to flee from the wrath to come and showing them the wonderful salvation in the love of Christ, our hearts rejoiced within us.

On Chinese New Year, the streets were filled with all kinds of people out to celebrate the holiday. After circulating thousands of tracts in the crowd, all the Adullam residents formed a circle on the street to preach the gospel. One of the older boys had prepared a sermon on a New Year's theme. But when he began preaching, the power of God fell so forcefully that this boy suddenly began speaking in other tongues while another person interpreted. One small boy after another took turns as interpreter. As soon as the Lord was through with one interpreter, he would step back and another would feel the anointing take his place. As soon as each boy stepped into the circle, he would immediately receive an interpretation.

These young boys hardly seemed like our boys when they preached under the anointing.

This went on for an hour or two as many people gathered to listen, jostling to get near enough to hear. They spoke with an earnestness so unusual that people who would seldom listen to the gospel now listened attentively. It was an evening conducted by the Holy Spirit in incredible order and beauty, each preacher being of the Lord's appointment, each one speaking a message from Him under direct inspiration. As we came away from that service, we seemed to understand what the preaching of the church was like in the beginning, and what the Lord wanted it to be in the end.

Not that preaching through other tongues and interpretation was to be the regular order of preaching, but, as 1 Corinthians 14 clearly shows, such preaching constitutes a part of the Lord's method of preaching the gospel in the power and demonstration of the Holy Spirit.

In such preaching the mind of the speaker is entirely disengaged. Often, before the words are formed, the speaker literally has no idea what the Spirit will speak through his lips. This is pure prophetic preaching.

In other cases, the mind of the speaker may be active and know before speaking (at least momentarily) what the Spirit will speak through him. The message may be an exposition of the Scriptures, as in the sermon by Stephen. Peter, on various occasions, preached as the Spirit spoke through him. Although preaching the gospel under the direct unction of the Holy Spirit is not exactly pure prophecy, it is nevertheless prophetic whenever the Holy Spirit directs and guides us.

The Lord was the guest preacher on several occasions in our little street chapel. For two or three nights, the youthful preachers, under the unction of the Spirit, preached the most inspiring sermons I have ever heard from Chinese evangelists. It seemed as if those sermons would stir anyone to repentance.

A few nights later, God showed His love in still greater power. A boy in his teens was preaching when suddenly his eyes closed and he began to prophesy like an Old Testament prophet under direct inspiration of the Holy Spirit. The manner of his preaching suddenly changed. The form of his Chinese language became rhythmic and perfect.

The manner of his speaking changed to the first person, such as, "I am the Lord God Almighty, the one true God, who made all things, who now speaks to you through this boy. Against Me you have sinned." I cannot fully describe to you the effect of these penetrating words, the sense of having been ushered into the presence of God. The seats of our little chapel were soon filled, with many more crowded around the door, listening in awe and wonder.

If there was the least commotion, the Lord commanded order, speaking through that boy and saying, "Make no mistake in this matter. Listen carefully and understand. I, the Lord God, have all the authority in heaven and on earth. To me every man and every demon must give account. I know all about every one of you. I know all your sins. I know how many hairs are on your head. There are fifty-six of you living in sin here tonight. Repent tonight, and I'll forgive you."

> Our little chapel was soon crowded with many who were listening in awe and wonder.

For half an hour or more we sat spellbound in the presence of a true prophet. The Lord rebuked people for idolatry, ungodliness, and all their vices until it seemed that there was no basis for hope left anywhere. Then, as in the case of the Old Testament prophets, God spoke of the glories He had prepared for His people. Like a loving father, He pleaded with them to repent that night. He spoke of the coming distress upon the nations and of the destruction of this ungodly race in the day of God's wrath. All these things were repeated several times along with exhortations to listen to every word as from a God who would hold every person present accountable for his own soul after that night.

When the prophecy was finished, the boy sat down. No one moved. There was not a single whisper. It seemed to me that every person must know that it was God who was speaking. Nearly all present had come in while the boy's eyes were shut. When the Lord spoke saying there were fifty-six present bound by the devil and sin, one of the boys carefully counted those not of our own Christian boys. There were just fifty-six.

"Demons Must Obey Me"

Another striking instance was that of a man from whom two demons were cast out. The Lord had told the boys through prophecy and direct revelation, "Demons must obey me," and they saw the Lord prove His word. Had we space to give details, we could prove beyond any other possible explanation that actual living demons were cast out of one devil-possessed man. We had known the man for a number of years, and he later stayed with us for six months. He had been the victim of melancholy and depression for many years. Because he was so bound in chains of darkness, he was ready to take his own life. To prevent this, we had kept him with us. He always seemed sad. All effort to lead him to any knowledge of salvation through Christ was of no avail. His mind was blind to everything pertaining to the blood of Christ.

The Lord used three people in casting out the demons. One demon, the size of a man, had an awful, black appearance. Several children saw him come out. While being rebuked by one suddenly *"filled with the Holy Spirit"* for that particular occasion, the demons put up a final fight for the man of their possession. The man's hands clenched together; his eyes shut tight; his whole body became rigid and resisting. Finally the Holy Spirit enlightened the man's heart; his body relaxed; his hands went up to God in praise.

> After he came out, the demon rushed about in great anger, seeking whom he might enter or tear.

Several children saw the demon after he came out, rushing about in great anger seeking whom he might enter or tear. All the children, having rushed in from where they had just sat down to their meal, stood about with uplifted hands, thanking and praising Jesus. Among these, the demon saw no opportunity, for they were all looking to Jesus whose blood covered them. The schoolteacher, who was not truly converted, also came in and was looking on in curiosity but was not praying. The angry demon, seeing his opportunity, seized this man and threw him to the floor with a thud. There the second demon sat upon him, so that the teacher could not rise. Several children saw this. Our gardener, who was some years ago mirac-ulously delivered from opium, saw this too. He was suddenly filled with the Holy Spirit and cast the demons out of the room.

> The physical appearance of the man from whom demons were cast out changed at once.

I saw only the two men, the one unbound and set free, the other fallen beside him. I supposed the schoolteacher was prostrated by the Holy Spirit of God, which was present in great power. I questioned him when he was able to rise as to why he wept and why he fell. He said, "I wept from sheer terror. Something awful happened. Everything became black; I saw myself about to go into a black pit at the base of a terrible mountain." When on the floor, he saw himself being bound by demon chains and about to be carried off into terrifying darkness, but he was set free again.

The physical appearance of the man from whom demons were cast out changed at once. He testified that he had peace and joy in his heart. He was given a vision of heaven at the time he was delivered from demons. When he lay in bed in the evening thinking about the Lord he became so happy that he wondered if it was right for him to have such great joy.

four

Visions of Heaven

Chapter 4

Visions of Heaven

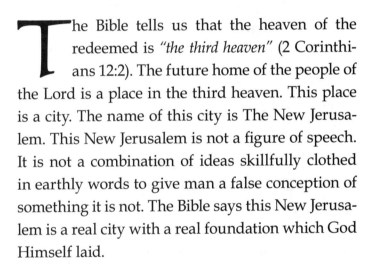

The Bible tells us that the heaven of the redeemed is *"the third heaven"* (2 Corinthians 12:2). The future home of the people of the Lord is a place in the third heaven. This place is a city. The name of this city is The New Jerusalem. This New Jerusalem is not a figure of speech. It is not a combination of ideas skillfully clothed in earthly words to give man a false conception of something it is not. The Bible says this New Jerusalem is a real city with a real foundation which God Himself laid.

This celestial city is foursquare, one thousand five hundred miles on every side, surrounded by a wall two hundred feet high with foundations of twelve kinds of precious stones, the most beautiful precious stones known to man. The wall itself is jasper, which sends forth a brilliant jasper light.

Twelve gates lead into the city, the streets of which are like gold. (See Revelation 21:11–12.) In this city are the homes of the redeemed, the abode of angels, paradise, and the throne of God.

Why shouldn't the New Jerusalem be a real city with streets of real gold and with jasper walls and with foundation stones of precious jewels? Did God so exhaust His material when He made the universe that He had no gold or jewels left for heaven? If God could make a world, could He not suspend a city in the sky beyond the stars? A little impure gold in this cursed and perverted earth, a precious jewel hidden in the debris of earthly ruins are only lingering reminders of the realities of which these are merely shadows. The real, the imperishable are in the city whose builder and maker is God.

> The New Jerusalem is a real city with a real foundation, which God Himself laid.

What we see on this perverted, degenerated earth are only shadows of the real thing. The creation *"was made subject to vanity"* (Romans 8:20) and unreality. The gold we cherish, the jewels we adore, the cities and mansions we build, are only copies of the real city that is soon coming down.

On the Streets of Heaven

The Adullam children were caught up in vision to this city of God. How they could see the city I do not know. How Abraham saw it I do not know. These things are beyond natural order. We need not, at present, know the how. We know the fact. John was shown the city. He was told by the Lord to write the things he had seen and send them to the churches.

In the Spirit, Adullam children were caught up to this city time after time, not as in a dream but as a living reality. Their visits were so real, in fact, that the children thought that their souls actually left their bodies to go to heaven and return. In some unaccountable way, they felt they had gone to heaven soul and body just as they might in daily life visit some distant destination. Frequently, when they were in paradise plucking and partaking of the heavenly fruit, they gathered some extra to tuck in their garments to bring back to earth for "Muh Si and Si Mu" (Pastor and Mrs. Baker).

They knew they were only on a visit to heaven and soon to return. Upon returning, when the Spirit lifted from them in our Adullam rooms, they proceeded at once to search in their pockets for the delicious fruit they had brought back to please us. Not finding this fruit, a look of great surprise, confusion, and disappointment came over their faces. They couldn't believe they had not gone to heaven in physical form and come back with the fruit tucked in their garments.

For the boys, the streets of New Jerusalem were as real as the streets of a Chinese city.

For them, walking on the streets of the New Jerusalem was as real as walking on the streets of a Chinese city. One day, when walking down our street in bright sunshine, I asked the boys if the visions were as real and as clear as what we were then seeing. "Just as real," they said, "but somehow much clearer due to the light in heaven and the white garments and the cleanliness everywhere, all adding to the brightness."

When in the Spirit, the children were usually oblivious to their natural surroundings. In many cases, although they supposed they were in heaven, they talked aloud, describing what they saw, thus carrying on a conversation that we all could hear. Often they acted out before our eyes what they were doing in heaven.

The Third Heaven

The Adullam children said they went to the third heaven. As they passed through the first heaven they felt air on their faces. Having passed the second heaven, they looked back upon the stars in their wonderful beauty, much as from a mountain height a person might gaze down upon a beautiful, light-studded city below.

Finally they reached the third heaven and came within sight of the New Jerusalem. As they approached this heavenly city they saw its light in the distance. Coming nearer, they saw the beautiful wall radiating its wonderful jasper light. The foundations were of indescribable beauty, sparkling with red, yellow, orange, purple, blue, green, violet, and the other colors of the twelve most beautiful jewels.

The children experienced this city in the sky as three cities in one; one city suspended above another, the largest city below, the smallest city on top, making a pyramid. Since John first described this city as surrounded by a wall, and since the city is one thousand five hundred miles high, Bible students have supposed the heavenly city is not a cube but a pyramid. Our children, however, knew nothing of this, neither had I ever thought of the New

Jerusalem as three cities, one suspended above another. Certainly God, who suspends the worlds in space, could suspend these cities in space. The Bible does not tell us the internal order of the city.

One of our small boys spoke in prophecy when in vision at the feet of the Lord. In this prophecy the Lord said that He had made heaven big enough for every living soul. He revealed that He had made it in three cities one above another, and that His throne is in the upper city.

Since time and distance are nothing in the heavenly realm, there is nothing impossible in such an arrangement of this city of God. There are three heavens. There were three stories in the ark, where God preserved the present creation. God is three in one. Why shouldn't the city of the Great King be three in one? Why shouldn't the King reign from the top of the pyramid of the entire universe, since *"the stone which the builders refused is become the head stone of the corner"* (Psalm 118:22), the capstone of the pyramid of all creation?

At Play with Angels

The children of Adullam entered by its pearly gates into the city of golden streets. Angels in white guarded the gates and welcomed them.

This was no beggarly reception. Here the once rejected off-scourings of the earth were welcomed as kings by these angelic hosts. Had not the Savior promised the weakest and humblest of these children a kingdom where they shall reign with the King of Kings for ages and ages?

Through the gates into the city! Out of earth into heaven! Out of the mortal into the immortal! Out of death into life! All the old life behind and below! All the new life ahead and above! Inside the gates! Angels, angels, everywhere—angels talking, angels singing, angels rejoicing, angels playing harps and blowing trumpets, angels dancing and praising the King. Such a scene no mortal has ever seen; such a flood of inner joy as no one ever knew flooded the whole being.

The once rejected off-scourings of the earth were welcomed as kings by these angelic hosts.

The children clapped their hands in rapture. They shouted for joy. They sometimes rolled on the floor in unrestrained laughter and jumped and danced in great delight, while their faces were so transformed by this heavenly joy that the glory of the celestial city seemed to shine upon us as well.

There was no sorrow in this city; no mournful, long-faced religion there; and no funeral dirges in the hymns. This was a city of joy, *"joy in the Holy Ghost"* (Romans 14:17), *"joy unspeakable and full of glory"* (1 Peter 1:8).

Inside the city, the children knew the meaning of the Scripture, which says, *"Ye are come unto mount Sion, and unto the city of the living God, the heavenly Jerusalem, and to an innumerable company of angels"* (Hebrews 12:22). Not only were these happy angels about the gates of the city, but also everywhere throughout the city. These heavenly hosts were always ready to escort the children from place to place throughout the city. Angels walked with them and talked with them; angels explained to them the meaning of things they did not understand, just as they had talked with John and revealed to him the things of God.

Often in these experiences with the angels, our children were given harps and taught to play them and sing as the angels did. They were also taught to blow the trumpets and were instructed in the music and language of heaven. When we saw the children, with closed eyes, all dancing about the room in rhythm, we found that in vision they were dancing with the angels in heaven and keeping time to the heavenly music. When we saw them apparently blowing a trumpet or going through the motions of playing a harp, we found that in vision they were joining the heavenly orchestra in the praises of the King. We could not see the heavenly harps or trumpets. We could not see the angels' joyful dance or hear their song. We could only hear the children singing heavenly songs.

It was a daily sight to find some child off in a corner by himself, lying comfortably on the pine needles, going through the motions of playing a harp. Upon going near, we could hear him sing-

> The climax of all heavenly joy and wonder was seeing Jesus and worshipping Him.

ing a new song we had never taught him. Approaching still nearer, we would discover that the words were as strange to us as the tune. The singer was singing in the heavenly choir. His song was one the angels taught him. The words of the song must have been in the language of angels. Seeing the children singing in this heavenly angelic choir was a sight not to be forgotten. Sometimes several of them, in some place in the heavenly city or its wonderful paradise, would decide to play and sing together. With closed eyes, while fully under the power of the Holy Spirit, three or four of them would get off by themselves. If we were near, we would hear a consultation as to who would play the trumpet and who would sing. After all was decided and everybody was ready, the heavenly hymns began. The trumpeters held their hands up before them and blew as though blowing trumpets. The harpists both played and sang, while those without instruments joined in the singing. In these cases they always sang in languages we did not understand, unless by mutual agreement they decided to sing one of those hymns they used to sing down on earth. In that case they sang in Chinese.

At the Throne of Christ

The climax of all heavenly joy and wonder was seeing Jesus and worshipping Him who had saved them by His blood. Soon after entering the gates of the city the children were escorted by the angels to go and see Jesus. We could hear these children talking about "going to see Jesus." When they came into His wonderful presence they stood reverently gazing with love and devotion upon the Lord of all creation, who was also their Savior. First, they thanked Him, adoringly worshipping Him and bowing in true obeisance. Then they knelt and bowed their faces to the floor to truly worship *"in spirit and in truth"* (John 4:23).

The throne of Christ the children saw was just as John described when he was in the Spirit:

And, behold, a throne was set in heaven, and one sat on the throne. And he that sat was to look upon like a jasper and a sardine stone: and there was a rainbow round about the throne, in sight like unto an emerald. And round about the throne were four and twenty seats: and upon the seats I saw four and twenty elders sitting, clothed in white raiment; and they had on their heads crowns of gold…and there were seven lamps of fire burning before the throne, which are the seven Spirits of God. (Revelation 4:2–5)

No matter how amazed the children were at the wonders of the golden city, no matter how happy in the pleasures of paradise, no matter how joyful in the presence of the angels, Jesus was never forgotten. His name was mentioned in all the conversation; His praise was mingled in all the enjoyments; He was always magnified everywhere, in everything, and in everybody there.

Our Heavenly Rooms

On either side of the beautiful golden streets were buildings side by side, a room for each person, every room opening onto the street. On the door and about the front were precious jewels so resplendently brilliant that the building shone with light and glory. The name of each occupant was above the door. Angels led the children into the rooms. Within all the rooms were the same kinds of furnishings: a beautiful golden table upon which was a Bible, a flower vase, a pen, and a book; by the table was a golden chair; there was also a wonderful golden chest and a golden bed. In each room was a jeweled crown, a golden harp, and a trumpet. The walls were gold. From each Bible, made of such paper as had never been seen on earth and was bound with gold and light, such brilliant glory shone forth that the whole room needed no other light. The visitors were told that when they came to stay after death they could go out into paradise and pick any flowers of their choice to place in the beautiful vase on the golden table.

> Each Bible was made of such paper as had never been seen on earth and was bound with gold and light.

In these visits to heaven, the children could go to their rooms at pleasure to read their Bibles or to play their harps and trumpets. Sometimes they took their trumpets or harps out into the streets or out into paradise to play and sing with the angels and the redeemed who were there in heaven.

In these excursions through heaven, the children, though lost to their real surroundings on earth, were always conscious that their visits to heaven were only temporary. They knew they were there only to see what was prepared for them after death, so they might go back to earth again and tell others. The angels and the Lord told their visitors that if they believed and obeyed all these things would be theirs. They not only knew they must come back to earth again, but they sometimes knew when they were coming.

One boy, after enjoying the glories of heaven, hung his crown and trumpet up in his room so they would be waiting for him when he would die and go to heaven to remain. He then came back to earth. The power of the Holy Spirit left him. When he opened his eyes he was in our Adullam room telling the wonders of this trip to heaven.

Are we to suppose that the Lord saved these boys, baptized them in the Holy Spirit, and then deceived them by showing them a figurative and mythical heaven? Impossible! An earthly father may deceive his children with false hopes and false promised, but our heavenly Father shows His children what He has for them (see 1 Corinthians 2:10), and promises He will give these things (see Revelation 3:21), and then gives the very things that He has promised. (See Luke 11:9, 13.)

When these children saw the heavenly rooms of their Adullam friends they clapped their hands, laughed, and shouted with great joy, calling each one by name to come and see his room. One of the boys was passing along the streets of New Jerusalem, reading the names above each door.

Seeing Those Who Had Gone Before

The first day when the Holy Spirit fell upon the children, one of the boys was caught up to heaven where he was welcomed by the angels and two Adullam boys who had died the year before. These two boys, Hsi Dien Fu and Djang Hsing, had with them in heaven a little girl who died in Kotchiu four years previously, and whom our children had forgotten.

Those who had died and gone on before led those who were caught up in the joys and wonders of heaven. They led them to see Jesus first of all, and to worship and thank Him. After this they were shown their dwellings and escorted around the city or led out into paradise to play.

All who went to heaven were given white garments. The angels, also dressed in seamless garments of spotless white, had wings, but the redeemed did not have wings. There was a clear distinction between the two.

Later on, many more of the children saw these former Adullam boys who were in heaven. Heaven did not seem far away as they acted out heavenly visions before our eyes. With closed eyes and radiant faces they clapped their hands and shouted for joy to these boys who died, calling them to hurry over to see some dwelling, some golden street, some new scene among the angels, some new discovery in the garden of paradise, or to come and play the harp and sing with them the praises of Jesus. These boys who had died were so constantly seen in heaven and their names were so frequently shouted in our midst with ecstasy and joy that they did not seem far away—just out of sight. Heaven was so real, so near, so wonderful, so certain, that if one of our children had died in

> Heaven was so real, so wonderful, that if one of our children had died, the others would have envied him his privilege.

those days, the others would have envied him his privilege.

The step to heaven after death or at the coming of the Lord seemed so small and the coming of the Lord so near that it removed from our minds all mystery as to why the first disciples could sell their possessions and face persecution and death without wavering.

Our kingdom is not of this world. Our citizenship is in heaven. Our life, our work, our service, our headships here are only brief and passing incidents on the way to the true life, the true city, in the true kingdom that cannot be shaken.

five

Paradise

Chapter 5

Paradise

B efore continuing to describe the visions of heaven, I wish to show that such a paradise as these children saw is in accordance with the Father's plans for us as revealed in His written Word. When the Lord created the first perfect man and his perfect bride, He *"planted a garden eastward in Eden"* (Genesis 2:8), in which he put the man whom he had formed. *"And out of the ground made the LORD God to grow every tree that is pleasant to the sight, and good for food; the tree of life also in the midst of the garden"* (verse 9). So, in the beginning the Lord planned for man to dwell in the middle of all the beauty of nature. He was given a home in the garden in the eastern part of Eden, a "wonder-park" that God Himself planned and planted.

In those days there was no sin. There was no sickness or death. There was no thorn or thistle.

There was no curse. That was a different world from this. That world was a heaven on earth with man enjoying what was meant to be eternal life, having dominion over a whole world of trees and flowers *"pleasant to the sight,"* a whole world of beauty and glory such as we have never seen. God planned all these wonders for man's eternal happiness.

But when sin entered, man's enjoyment of this creation became a limited, temporal enjoyment. The first creation of birds, flowers, trees, and animals fell into a lower order that is not eternal. Creation *"was made subject to vanity"* (Romans 8:20). Sin caused man to lose his Eden "park" and his Eden God.

After God's plan of redemption is completed and man is restored from sin, then man will be restored to his Eden God and his Eden "park," But man will be restored to more than the primal order; he will be restored to the new spiritual order.

The first order was earthly; the last order will be spiritual but real. The spiritual order is similar to the earthly. Jesus, after His resurrection, was both real and similar to what He was before but was still spiritual and different from the earthly order. He could still eat and drink with His disciples. He still had flesh that could be felt and hands that could serve fish and bread to His hungry disciples. But in the resurrected order, the Lord was not subject to the limitations of the physical, material world of time and space. Even so, the world with its natural order of animal, bird, and plant creation is to be born again into a higher, spiritual dimension similar to the first creation but also different from it. It will be the real order not again subject to corruption and unreality.

All of Creation in Eternity

The natural creation is to be born again through the resurrection of Christ. Yet Christ saves more than just man. He saves the entirety of creation that fell into unreality at the fall of man.

> *For the earnest expectation of the creature* [creation] *waiteth for the manifestation of the sons of God. For the creature* [creation] *was made subject to vanity, not willingly, but by reason of him who hath subjected the same in hope, because the creature* [creation] *itself also shall be delivered from the bondage of corruption into the glorious liberty of the children of God.*
>
> (Romans 8:19–21)

If this does not mean that the present natural order of plant, animal, and all natural life looks forward to being set free by the resurrection power of Jesus, then what does it mean? All nature looks forward to the new spiritual regeneration that belongs to the redeemed, for Christ *"begat He us with the word of truth, that we should be a kind of first-fruits of His creatures"* (James 1:18).

Christ Himself *"is the image of the invisible God, the first-born of every creature"* (Colossians 1:15). How is Christ *"the first-born of every creature"* unless it is that in His resurrection into the new order, animal and plant creation will eventually follow as the full harvest? Christ was but the *"firstfruits."* Even the earth itself is to be regenerated in the new order, since *"we, according to His promise, look for new heavens and a new earth, wherein dwelleth righteousness"* (2 Peter 3:13). Will not that new earth have trees and flowers and animals and birds and all the beauties of glorified nature in a higher indestructible order that will last forever?

> *The wolf also shall dwell with the lamb, and the leopard shall lie down with the kid; and the calf and the young lion and the fatling together; and a little child shall lead them.* (Isaiah 11:6)

> All nature looks forward to the new spiritual regeneration that belongs to the redeemed.

These things are as certain as the word of God, for *"he that sat upon the throne said, Behold, I make all things new. And he said unto me, Write: for these words are true and faithful"* (Revelation 21:5).

John *"saw the holy city, new Jerusalem, coming down from God out of heaven"* (Revelation 21:2) to the *"new earth"* (v. 1.)

As there was an Eden-park of delight on the first earth, so also, in a higher, regenerated, resurrected order, the New Jerusalem will contain an Eden-park on the new earth in the new order. This Eden-park is already in heaven in the New Jerusalem that has not yet descended, but is soon coming down.

Realities of Paradise

Perhaps the revelation of such a paradise in heaven as the children of Adullam saw will be as new to most of the readers as it was to us. This is because we are so dull of mind and slow to believe all that is written in the scriptures.

We did not teach these children about this paradise. The children taught us. Some of the smallest children, who were naturally most ignorant of these matters, were our best teachers. That they got these things from the Lord is clearly evident, as you will see by a comparison with the teaching of the Bible. It teaches there is just such a paradise in heaven as these children saw. Paul said he knew a man who was *"caught up to the third heaven"* (2 Corinthians 12:2) and that this person *"was caught up into paradise"* (verse 4). In the messages of Revelation, the Spirit says to the churches, *"to him that overcometh will I give to eat of the tree of life, which is in the midst of the paradise of God"* (Revelation 2:7). We are also told that *"on either side of the river, was there the tree of life, which bare twelve manner of fruits"* (Revelation 22:2). So there is indeed a paradise with flowing water and trees of fruit.

This paradise is a great "park" of surpassing wonder, and that is just what the word *paradise* means. *Paradise* means "Eden." *Eden* means "paradise." Eden is a park; paradise is, therefore, a park. *Peloubet's Bible Dictionary* says of *paradise*: "This is a word of Persian origin, and is used in the Septugint as the translation of 'Eden.' It means an orchard of pleasure and fruits, a garden, or pleasure ground something like an English park."

But this park in heaven is only something like a park on earth, because it is far greater than earthly parks in extent and beauty. Man's most beautiful parks, with their picturesque landscapes, flowing streams, crystal pools, wooded nooks, verdant greens, fragrant variegated flowers, caroling birds, and playful pets, are only imperfect imitations on the part of man to reproduce the Eden that was *"in the beginning."*

If God did not put into the heart of man this love for nature and this desire for natural parks of pleasure and fruit, then how do you account for this universal love of nature that has been in the heart of man from the days of his earliest history? Are all man's efforts to preserve a little of the vanishing natural beauties of this cursed and perishing earth only a vain fancy to be followed for a few fleeting years? Is our love for birds, animals, flowers, trees, mountains, valleys, lakes, streams, and all this handiwork of God just a passing amusement given by the Lord to cheer us a little on this weary journey? Are not the finest combinations of all that is beautiful in nature just a mere foreshadowing of the unlimited realities in the paradise of God in heaven?

Scenes of natural beauty are God's guideposts, pointing to the Eden at the end of our way.

These natural beauties are not just scenes along the way. Rather, they are guideposts of God, pointing to the Eden of beauty at the end of the way. Love of nature may become an eternal love, enlarged beyond all natural limits for all who overcome by the blood of the Lamb, who, by faith in him, enter by the gates into the city whose beauty will never be marred by sin.

I am sure you will be interested, as we were, in what else our Adullam children saw in the paradise, the Eden, in the city beyond the sky. One of the young men was in paradise almost as soon as he entered the heavenly city. He was met there by the two Adullam boys who had died in Hokow. These boys, taking him through paradise and the other parts of the holy city, soon came to a great, lawn-like grassy, open plot surrounded by magnificent trees.

The whole scene was so entrancing that the young man said to his two glorified friends, "this is good enough for me. There can't be anything more beautiful. I'll stay right here."

The boys who had preceded him to heaven said, "No, don't wait here, for there are much greater marvels."

Going on a little farther they came to still more wonderful trees, some of them bearing fruit. The whole park-like surroundings and the grassy lawn beneath the trees were enticing beyond any earthly understanding.

The young man said, "I must stay here, I cannot go on and leave this great beauty. I am so happy."

"Come on," said the others, "there are many things in heaven exceeding this."

"You go," he replied, "but I shall remain right here for awhile."

The others left him on the grass under the trees with the great, open, velvet-like grassy space before him. Floods of joy and happiness he had never known on earth flooded his whole being. He was in the land of joy, "the land that is fairer than day."

> The park-like surroundings and grassy lawn beneath the trees were enticing beyond any earthly understanding.

Frequently an angel came walking by, playing a harp and singing. The angel smiled, offered him the harp. "I cannot play," he said. The angel passed by. Soon other angels came, smiling to him as they played and sang.

The angels were dressed in seamless garments of white; their faces were perfect; one was not more beautiful than another. "When they smiled—Oh, I can't describe that," the boy said later, "there is no way on earth to describe an angel's smile."

Similar and surpassingly beautiful scenes in paradise were seen repeatedly by a large number of Adullam children. In paradise they saw trees bearing the most delicious fruit, and vistas of the most beautiful flowers of every color, sending forth an aroma of heavenly fragrance. There were birds of glorious plumage singing their carols of joy and praise. In this park were also animals of every size and description: large deer, small deer, large lions, great elephants, lovely rabbits, and all sorts of little friendly pets such as they had never seen before.

The children held the little pets in their arms and passed them from one to another. They found the lion peacefully lying beneath a tree and climbed on his back, ran their fingers through his shaggy mane, brushed his face, and put their hands in his mouth. If they desired, they curled down beside him to enjoy together the love of their common Maker. Why not? *The wolf also shall dwell with the lamb, and the leopard shall lie down with the kid; and the calf and the young lion and the fatling together; and a little child shall lead them...their young ones shall lie down together* (Isaiah 11:6–7).

The little children rode the small deer, while the other children rode the larger deer or the friendly elephant. All was perfect love. All was great harmony. Such shouts of joy! Such happy childish laughter! Who but our Father in heaven could have ever thought of or planned such a paradise?

When hungry, the children ate of the wonderful fruit or gathered freely the sweet tasting, refreshing manna that was scattered all about. Were they thirsty? Here and there trickled little brooks of the stimulating and refreshing water of life.

Such visions strengthen and confirm our faith in the Word of God and its promise of eternal life through Christ Jesus.

In the open, lawn-like vistas amidst the trees and flowers and birds of paradise, the children of Adullam saw companies of the redeemed dancing and playing trumpets with the angels. Sometimes they joined this happy, festive group, in which were small children, larger children, and adults, but where no one was old. What heavenly scenes! What heavenly singers! What joy among the angels and the redeemed! The angels pointed out Abraham, David, and Daniel, the prophets, the saints, and the martyrs of old. They saw Peter, James, Paul, and others of whom the world was not worthy. Our boy from the poor Miao tribe saw his aunt and his own little sister who had gone ahead to paradise. Taking our boys by the hand our little Chinese Mary, who died in Kotchiu, now also joined them in heaven.

What Happens at Death

I well remember how one of our boys was given a vision of what happens at the death of a Christian. As relatives and friends gathered about the dying one, an angel stood by the bed awaiting the liberation of the Christian's soul. When the man was set free from his bodily encumbrance, the angel took him by the arm and ascended with him into heaven. The principalities and powers of evil hosts in mid-heaven in their attempts to hinder the passage of the angel and his charge were overcome by the angels' faith and praise as the ascent continued toward the heavenly city.

Having been welcomed at the gate, this new arrival was received by hosts of angels, singing, dancing, rejoicing, all uniting in giving him a royal welcome into the eternal city of the redeemed.

Such visions as these have but confirmed our faith in the Word of God and its promise of eternal life through Christ Jesus.

six

Angels in Our Midst

Chapter 6

Angels in Our Midst

Outpourings of the Holy Spirit upon the Adullam youth were always attended with visions of angels in our midst.

In this connection it is well to remember some scriptural teaching about angels. The Scriptures teach that angels have a part in the ministration of the Holy Spirit. Since *"the spirits* [or angels] *of the prophets are subject to the prophets"* (1 Corinthians 14:32), angels have some part in prophetic utterance when a prophet speaks under the inspiration of the Holy Spirit. The visions John saw on Patmos and the revelations he had there when he was *"in the Spirit"* were given him through an angel. (See Revelation 1:1, 10.) Angels, therefore, have something to do with being in a trance, seeing visions through the Holy Spirit, and getting revelations through the Holy Spirit.

Angelic Ministry

Each true church has, perhaps, a special angel to minister to that particular church. (See Revelation 1:20.) Every saved person has an angel to minister to him. (See Hebrews 1:14; Acts 12:15.) Every child has the ministry of angels, for the angels of children have constant access to the throne of God in heaven. (See Matthew 18:10.) Angels always see us, though we seldom see angels. Angels differ in rank. (See 1 Corinthians 4:9.)

Apparently, angels have a part in saving the lost.

Both the Old and New Testaments furnish sufficient proof for the reality of angelic ministry in the Adullam Home. We have already told of the visions of angels rescuing people whom demons had bound with awful chains and were dragging to hell. Angels, then, apparently have a part in saving the lost. Since angels led these children to heaven and escorted them through the golden streets and the glories of paradise, it seems that angels had something to do with the visions given to the children of Adullam. As most of the children who spoke in other languages did so when they were dancing and singing with the angels, it may be that angels have something to do with speaking in other languages, for it is possible to speak with *"the tongues of...angels"* (1 Corinthians 13:1) at times of mighty outpourings of the Spirit.

The children also had wonderful visions of multitudes of angels flying in the heavens, and sometimes they saw them fly from heaven to earth.

At the times when the presence of the Holy Spirit was especially manifest many of the children saw angels near or in the room. When they were hindered by demonic power they saw angels come to their release. On occasions of the most blessed sense of the presence of the Lord in our midst and of the sweetest harmony and love in the meeting, just above the room was a large angel, while the room was entirely surrounded by smaller angels standing side by side, each touching the other to the right and left, so there was not a space in the whole circle for the entrance of any demon. On these occasions, when one or more of the children saw our angel garrison about us, there were never any visions of demons in the room as

> The children had wonderful visions of multitudes of angels flying in the heavens.

were often seen at other times. One evening when our angel guard was about us in such perfect rank, children said they could hear demons outside the circle of angels making an angry commotion because of their inability to hinder the blessed fellowship in the Holy Spirit that was within the angels' circle. Boys in Kotchiu had also seen this circle of angels.

I shall never forget the blessed sense of the very presence of God that was in those meetings in which the children saw the angel just above our happy, Spirit-filled people. This angel looking down upon us, smilingly turned from side to side to look at the angels that encircled us and to see that there was not an entrance for the powers of darkness. I wondered if the angel above us was not the special angel of Adullam and if the smaller angels of lesser rank around us were not our individual guardians. At any rate, the children saw the angels. Their eyes were usually closed when they saw them, but sometimes they saw them with wide-open eyes. We could believe, without question, that we were indeed in the presence of angels.

seven

The Kingdom of the Devil

Chapter 7

The Kingdom of the Devil

No careful observer could have been with us during those weeks of the mighty outpouring of the Holy Spirit and doubted that there are two kingdoms that are in constant conflict. As surely as angels minister and the Holy Spirit leads to a real kingdom of light, so surely do demons hinder, while the devil presides in a realm of evil spirits in a kingdom of real darkness. Through these visions, one kingdom was made as certain to us as the other. And man was clearly revealed as the battleground.

The Bible teaches that there are lower and higher ranks of evil spirits and that our conflict is *"not against flesh and blood, but against principalities, against powers, against the rulers of the darkness of this world, against spiritual wickedness in high places"* (Ephesians 6:12). Both

Old and New Testaments teach the reality of a kingdom of darkness and the reality of demons.

I related how demons were cast out of one man and how the larger demon was seen to rush about the room in great anger, finally seizing upon an unguarded schoolteacher who was looking on, and throwing him to the floor. In this instance, two boys saw this big, black, man-like demon enter the man of his possession. After this demon had been cast out and chased out of the room by a Spirit-filled young man, several children saw him take temporary refuge behind some small trees in our courtyard. This demon was accompanied by another about half his size. Both demons were seen by children who were praying. Some children were praying with eyes closed and some with eyes opened. But all saw the same things at the same time. The appearance of the demons was identical with each individual.

Confronting Demons

In the Adullam Rescue Home we had a young girl who was evidently open to demon activity. She said that before coming here she was subject to "fits," or spells of unconsciousness. A short time after she arrived, she and some of the younger girls were on a walk outside the city. On the way back, one of the new girls, who was half-blind and some-what slow, lingered behind and lost her way. The older girl, having gone to find the one who was lost, was returning home with her when she saw three demons before her, a few steps away. One was "as tall as a door" and was accompanied by two others about the size of a boy twelve years old. All these demons were dark in appear-ance, with big eyes and awful faces. The two smaller demons, being apparently subject to the large one, obeyed and followed him. The girl was frightened

> When there were manifestations that we did not understand, we kept praying and trusting the Lord.

at what she saw. The large demon, coming near, seized her by the head. She became dizzy, almost unconscious, and could scarcely walk. She could hardly see the street and had to be led home by the other girl whom she had gone to seek.

Upon reaching home she was better for a time. A little later, while we were at supper, someone came in saying that the afflicted girl was in her room unconscious. We found her prostrate on the floor, breathing as if in peaceful sleep, but we could not awaken her. After praying for her we all assembled in the regular evening prayer meeting. Soon the girl came in perfectly well.

She said that she seemed to be bound by chains and dragged by demons farther and farther down a great dark road, while all the time she was silently praying; then she suddenly realized that the Lord had set her free and she was able to rise. At once she became conscious, and her mind clear. As she sat on her bed alone in the room, she saw the three demons that she had met on the street now in the room. But now she felt no fear, for she knew that the Lord was Conqueror. Accordingly, she drove the demons out of the room in "the name of Jesus." As they reluctantly receded step by step she followed in the name of Jesus until she drove them along the walk and out of the large Chinese door at the entrance of our compound. In the several succeeding months that she was there she had no more "fits" or unconscious spells.

Overcoming Fear of Demons

When there were manifestations that we did not understand, we kept praying and trusting the Lord but decided not to interfere unless we clearly saw something that was harmful or sinful. After eight weeks of wonderful manifestations of the

Holy Spirit, we were most thankful that we had allowed such liberty among the children. We saw how marvelously the Lord had led them, and things we did not understand at first proved to be part of the Lord's plan in giving us some of the most wonderful and precious revelations.

While some of the children were having a blessed time in the Holy Spirit, others went to sleep when they tried to pray. Those under the anointing often saw demons by those who were drowsy and could not pray through. They saw demons coming in through the open window or the door. Sometimes they saw demons lazily reclining under the table or upon a couch that was in the room. Under the anointing of the Holy Spirit, the children, with closed eyes, in the name of Jesus, would rout the demons out of their places and follow them until they went out of the door or window.

They frequently followed these demons out of the room, opened a front or back door to the compound, and chased the demons off the premises. When demons appeared on the scene, they were often seen by several persons at the same time.

Some of the children had seen demons before. We found that in spite of all our teaching about the Lord they were still so afraid of demons, they dared not go to their rooms alone at night, and they covered their heads when they slept. Through these revelations, however, the children found that the largest and fiercest demons were ineffective against even the smallest child who was covered by Jesus' blood, so that, for the first time, we had a happy lot of Chinese children who had lost their fear of demons, were not afraid in the dark, and were not afraid to sleep with uncovered heads.

> The largest and fiercest demons were ineffective against even the smallest child who was covered by Jesus' blood.

The demons seen were best described as resembling the demonic idols in Chinese temples. According to the Bible, and according to the Chinese, much idolatry is demon worship. Making idols of the demon type is an attempt to reproduce the likeness of demons that have been seen.

The children saw demons as "high as a door," with pointed chins and warty heads. There were others of different appearance too, some half this size. There were smaller ones, two or three feet high, and little ones only a few inches high who followed the larger demons about.

The large, bug-eyed, fierce-looking demons were the ones to be feared as having the power to bind and take captives to hell. The hosts of the powers of the air and their works of darkness, in cooperation with demons on earth, were seen by various Adullam witnesses, whose testimony is as follows:

The government of the hosts of evil is in mid-heaven. There are thrones from which the devil's angels exercise their satanic government over the earth. These rulers of darkness vary. Some are larger in stature than others; there is variation in dress, crowns, facial expression, disposition, and authority. In all respects they are as devilish in appearance and acts as the hosts of Satan are expected to be.

These rulers of evil are in constant contention amongst themselves, each resenting the authority of those higher in power, each jealous of the other and all covetous of the seats of highest rank. Those in higher rank hold their positions, not by consent of the lower orders, but solely through their own superior fierceness and power. Cliques and individuals are in constant conflict and quarrels.

All have crowns that represent various orders and ranks. All desire to sit on the thrones above and supervise the work of evil on earth, rather than descend to earth on delegated duties to further the demonical powers below.

Those of highest rank sit on thrones in the mid-heavens, ruling over innumerable hosts of evil spirits, from whose number delegations are constantly dispatched to earth to entice its inhabitants, to withstand the forces of righteousness, to strengthen weak places in the demonical forces of earth, and to bind and to drag the souls of evil men to hell when they die.

Although these wicked demons fly in high heaven to the very gates of the New Jerusalem and although they descend to earth and fly in its air, the center where they congregate in countless numbers is in the region of the thrones of authority in the mid-heavens. Here evil hosts of wicked spirits of all sizes fly hither and thither or move about more deliberately. A certain halo surrounds the wicked angels of higher rank.

All are similar in some respects: all have wings, all have crowns, and all belong in the heavens. The delegated messengers go to earth only temporarily. Their evil errand finished, they again returned to the heavens.

The hosts of evil spirits on earth are very different from those, which fly through the heavens.

Those on earth do not have wings; they can walk and run rapidly; and they move freely but apparently do not leave the earth. They vary in size from a few inches to ten feet in height, wear gaudy colored clothes of many stripes, and have fancy caps of various shapes and colors; some, on the other hand, wear rags or filthy garments.

Some of these demons on earth have very little power and are of a rather harmless order. Others, however, are large in stature, fierce in appearance, and have great power. These on earth withstand the work of righteous men and the work of angels among them. In one of their conflicts with an angel, earthly demons

> Suddenly, the glory of God descended and entirely routed all the hosts of evil.

of highest rank, assisted by others of lower rank, gathered about the angel, trying to strike him with clubs, swords, and other weapons. Through faith and praising the Lord, the angel so withstood this onslaught that no blow fell upon him nor could an evil hand touch him. The demons of lesser power, standing at a little distance and watching the conflict, upon seeing their companions unsuccessful in their attack, besought the powers of evil in the heavens to send a reinforcement of the devil's angels from the air. In response to this entreaty, a detachment of ten was sent down. As these approached the earth the demons below clapped their hands in joyous welcome. When the demons from above reached the scene of conflict, these less powerful demons, receding a distance, stood in respectful quietness in the presence of the Satanic delegation from above, who now took up the conflict with the angel. These forces the angel also withstood with praises and faith until suddenly the glory of God descended and entirely routed all the hosts of evil.

Visions of Dying

The same boy who saw the vision of the Christian dying also saw a vision of what happens at the death of an unbeliever. He saw a man wandering about unhindered from place to place on earth, until one of the devil's angels, descending from the sky with chains, bound him and forced him down to hell.

Another boy saw a vision of the death of a professing Christian who had known the Lord, but had not truly repented. This was even more terrible. When this man was dying, demons by his deathbed waited in fiendish delight for the liberation of the soul of this hypocritical, one-time professing Christian. The demons began to bind him before he was entirely out of the body and completed the binding of their captive the minute he drew his last ungodly breath. The hypocrite did not enjoy one moment of freedom to wander about the earth. An object of ridicule to his demon captors, in terror he was at once dragged and pushed into hell.

One such ungodly man became the special sport of demons who, having bound him in chains, dragged him along on the earth, again and again jerking him up on his feet only again to drag him down and haul him along like a dead dog. After furnishing amusement for his captors, the man was dragged down the dark road to the infernal regions.

The Thief

At this point, I would like to tell you about one of our boys who had been discharged as errand boy by an officer in the army. After seeing him begging on the street for several days we took him into the Adullam Rescue Home. He promised to reform, made an outward showing of decency, heard the gospel for a considerable time, and professed repentance.

Different items disappeared from the Home, but the thief was not found until this boy was caught on his way to sell the stolen plunder. We then put him out of the House.

After several months of beggar life, during which time this boy repeatedly promised to reform if only we would allow him to return, we gave him another chance. The Lord also gave him another chance, for there were visible manifestations of the Holy Spirit and supernatural revelations occurring sufficient to make the way of life clear to even the most stubborn sinner. This boy himself experienced the anointing of the Holy Spirit, when the Lord dealt directly with him about his sins and showed him the better way.

Visible manifestations of the Holy Spirit occurred sufficient to make the way of life clear to even the most stubborn sinner.

In spite of all this, the boy ran away and joined a street gang of beggar-thieves. A few months later he fell and broke his arm and eventually infection set in. He was close to death when a hospital worker picked him up. In the hospital, he was so hopelessly disobedient that he was thrown out and was soon left to die on the street. Coming to us with promises of repentance, we pitied him and took him in once more.

Day by day he grew worse and worse. The night before he died, I was awakened by unearthly shrieks that sounded like uncanny howls of some wild animal. The next day when the boy died, I was away from home. As he lay in death throes, delighted, awful hellish demons gathered about him. When his soul was leaving his body the boy, seeing his captors, wept, yelled, shrieked, and cried at the top of his voice in wildest terror, "Mr. Baker, help! Help! Help! Oh, Mr. Baker, come quickly! Mr. Baker, Mr. Baker! Help, they are all about me with chains! They have come for me. Help, help, Mr. Baker, help! Oh, oh, help! Help! They are binding me with chains. Help! Help! Oh, oh, oh, help! Oh—h-e-l-…"

Realities of Hell

Over and over again the children had visions of hell and the lake of fire. The first time anyone was under the anointing of the Spirit, he usually had a vision of hell. Typically, he was bound in chains by demons and taken through a region of darkness. Some children could hear demons all about them in this region. If taken far, they could see a dim light in the distance, which proved to be reflections from the lake of fire. Some children were forced so near they could see the lake of fire ahead. All the time they were pleading the blood of Christ, asserting that they would not obey and would not be subject to the slavery of their captors. They believed Jesus would surely save. We have already told how at this climax, before the lake of fire was reached, the Lord did intervene with His blood-bought salvation.

The Bible pictures hell as a place of blackness and darkness, and it teaches that part of the devil's angels are now reserved in chains of darkness awaiting judgment.

The children saw not only darkness in hell, but also the lake of fire, which was always approached through a region of stygian darkness. In their vision they were led to the edge of a great lake of molten fire in a semi-dark pit from which arose clouds of smoke. When the smoke settled low, the fire in the lake was less distinct. When the smoke lifted a little, the burning lake with red and greenish flames and its inmates could be distinctly seen.

When the children were peering down into this pit in hell we saw them taking a firm hold on some piece of furniture or, getting down on their hands and knees, cautiously bending forward to peer into the infernal regions. They would look for a moment and then drew back, afraid lest they fall in. They were horrified at what they saw. Then, very cautiously, they looked again and drew back. Sometimes the children lay flat on their stomachs, lest they slip and fall while looking over the brink of the lake of fire.

The lost were seen going into hell. Some fell in, some walked over the brink, and some were bound by demonic chains and cast into hell. One boy saw groups of the wicked bound in bundles, ready to be cast into this furnace of fire.

Coming out of the lake of fire were oceans of hands reaching up for help.

When the fire abated and the smoke settled down, the moans of those in misery could be heard. Whenever the fire would increase in intensity and the smoke would lift a little, there were shrieks and wails of agony.

In the lake of fire were oceans of hands reaching up for help. Those below pled with those looking in upon them to come to their rescue. Those of us witnessing these children in the midst of their vision heard our children talking to them as clearly as you can hear someone talking over the telephone and get but one end of the conversation. We could hear one end of a conversation like this:

"I can't help you."

"No, I cannot do anything for you."

"But when you were alive you would not obey the gospel."

"No, it is too late; before you got here I preached to you, but you made fun of me and despised Jesus. Now you know I told you the truth."

"No, I cannot do anything; this is the judgment of God."

"If you had obeyed, you would now be enjoying heaven with us."

After some such conversation, mercifully, the children were led away to enjoy the presence of Jesus in heaven or the glories of the golden streets of the paradise of God.

We are told in the Bible that Lazarus could see the rich man in hell tormented in flames, and the rich man could talk with Lazarus, but he could not cross the gulf. When Christ reigns as King of Kings upon the earth, the redeemed nations will look upon the lost.

One boy saw his grandmother in hell whom he had tried to win to Christ. She was once a sorceress and murderer who had withstood the gospel she had heard in her village. She had caused many to refuse the light. Other children also had visions of relatives in hell.

There was no vision of anyone in heaven or the name of any one on the mansions by the golden streets who did not trust in Jesus. Those in hell were all unbelievers. One night the Lord spoke through a small boy in wonderful prophecy.

Among the things he said was, "There will be no one in heaven except those who believe in the gospel."

After the Lord had taken the boys and girls through the most wonderful and systematic lessons in the Holy Spirit, they nearly all came at last to the parting of the roads. In this vision, repeated until it seemed the impression could never be forgotten, the one in the vision seemed to be standing by the cross at the parting of the two great roads. One was the narrow way of life that leads to heaven and glory; the other was the broad way to hell and destruction.

Great, busy, hurrying multitudes—multitudes hustling with business, carrying great loads of sin and rushing along with the affairs of life—were passing in endless streams and countless numbers. The child was the preacher at the crossroads. Again we heard one side of the conversation:

Hello, my friend! Please wait a minute; I want to speak to you. Say, do not go down that broad road; it leads to hell and ruin. I have been down that way and have seen hell for myself. Stop here by the cross and let Jesus wash all your sins away. From the cross of Christ here you can start up this other road that will lead you to heaven and everlasting life and joy.

Oh! That fellow does not believe it. There he goes on down the broad road. What a pity! I will stop this other man and see if he will believe.

Hey there! Just a minute! Say, do not follow that crowd. They do not know where they are going. That road leads to destruction; that is the road to the lake of fire. Please don't go on. I came out here to stop as many of you as possible and give you fair warning. Better turn aside here, let Jesus wash your sins away, and go with us up the road to heaven where God is. Oh, there he goes, too!

Here is another. Wait a moment! Say, come out of that crowd. Can't you see there is no one returning? They all go down that road and no one ever comes back. That is the broad road to hell. Stop here by the cross, believe the gospel of salvation through Jesus' blood, and you will be safe. There is no other road further on. This is the only road to heaven. Turn in here or you will be lost too. Oh, what a pity he does not believe me. There he goes with the others.

Sometimes the youthful preacher would decide that if no one believed him, he would follow the willful crowd to see what happened.

When he arrived with the crowd at the brink of the lake of fire in hell, we heard him say, "Look at that crowd falling into hell! Not one escapes. Everyone goes in."

Slowly drawing near the edge of the pit and leaning over and looking down into the lake with its suffering multitudes, the preacher said: "I cannot help you now. I told you all about this back there at 'The Gospel Crossroads,' but you would not believe. And you still would not believe, even if I could help you out. No, I am helpless now. If you had listened when I warned, the Lord would have saved you; you came on and fell in because you would not take advice. No, I can't. I am going back to the Crossroads to see if I can find someone who will listen. I must stop a few at any cost."

He was occasionally successful in persuading one to listen. Then he would say, "Now, you get down there at the foot of the cross of Jesus and pray, 'Jesus, I am a sinner. I was on my road to hell. I am only fit for hell. The big load I carry is only sin. Forgive my sins and teach me to live only for Your glory. Amen.'"

> There was great rejoicing as the sinner was saved and started up the narrow road.

There was rejoicing then as the sinner was saved and started up the narrow road, while the preacher went out to try to rescue another deluded traveler.

These visions, with some variations, were repeated many times, making it clear that salvation was only by repentance and belief in the blood of Christ, through the preaching of the gospel; that many were called; that few were saved; that the road to destruction is broad and multitudes pass that way; that the way of life is narrow and few are those who find it. It was made equally clear that the Christian is to stand in the gap at the parting of the ways and persuade and warn to the limit of his ability.

We have told how the boys, even the small boys, went out at that time and preached on the streets with unction of the Holy Spirit, sometimes under direct inspiration such as we had never before witnessed. I will close this chapter with the story of the university student who went by the Crossroads.

Opposite our front gate lived a university student who was to have graduated from the university that year. I talked with him, asking him to come over and discuss the Bible and Christianity in a friendly way. He came a few days, and I felt certain he was convinced of the truth of what I said. The questions he raised seemed to be answered to his full satisfaction.

Through him I managed to get a chance to talk with some of the other university students during their vacation. (It was during this time that we experienced the mighty outpouring of the Holy Spirit at Adullam.) The students were friendly, and I felt that my original student friend saw clearly the truth of the gospel. But, although he was polite, he was not inclined to accept the truth and did not seem to like the friendly way the other students responded to the Bible discussions.

One morning when one of our girls was out at our front gate, it happened that this young university student was out there too. The girl began telling him he ought to be a Christian, in a simple way urging him to believe in Jesus to save him from his sins, to make him a good man, to save him from hell, and to lead him to heaven.

"What's the use of my being a Christian?" he said. "I do not need to be saved."

"You might die suddenly in your sins," the girl replied, "and you would go to hell."

"Who are you?" scoffed the student. "You are a little snip of an ignorant girl, just a sort of useless beggar. What do you suppose you are trying to do? You are trying to teach me something when you are not worthy to even talk to me. I am a university student. I am wise. I have read many books. I have been many years in Peking. I can speak and read English as well as Chinese." Then he spit in her face and told her to mind her own business.

Two weeks later, I heard the sounds of a funeral procession in the front alley. I was surprised to learn that they were carrying this university student to his burial; I had seen him on the street just a few days before. One of the boys said that as we were going out to preach a few days earlier, he had offered this young student a tract, but the student would not take it.

I knew nothing of this conversation with the girl. About a month later she was under the power of the Spirit. After seeing visions of heaven and the glories of the redeemed, she stood still and bent over as though looking into hell.

These things taught us to believe more assuredly than ever in the reality of heaven and hell.

This is what I heard:

Ah! There is hell. No, I cannot; I have no power to help you now. You certainly are in an awful plight. It is you who are worse than a beggar now; all dirty, all filthy, and suffering in the lake of fire. In fact, you look worse now than any beggar I ever saw. I thought you told me you were wise and that you had a great education. Where is your education now? Well, I cannot help you now even if you do apologize. That may be, but I have no power. No, only Jesus can save you, but when I told you about Him you made fun of Him and cursed me. Look what we beggars who believe in Jesus have received in heaven: all is joy, all is happiness, all is love in the city of golden streets with its wonderful paradise of God.

Then the girl seemed to be crossing the lake of fire over a narrow bridge. We saw her walking as though she were walking on a tightrope, placing one foot carefully in front of the other while extending her arm on either side until she recovered her balance.

With a sigh of relief she said, "My! This is dangerous! But the Lord will help me. I will get across to the other side." Then she carefully brought the other foot forward and nearly lost her balance again. She praised the Lord until she recovered her balance and proceeded as before. In this way having crossed the room, she seemed to be safely in heaven, past every danger of ever falling into the lake of fire.

Whatever the effect of relating these visions may have on others, these things taught us in Adullam to believe more assuredly than ever in the reality of heaven and the kingdom of God, and in the reality of hell and the kingdom of the devil. More positively than ever do we assert that the way through this life that leads over the dangers of the lake of fire, the way that overcomers must travel, is like walking a rope which must be traveled step by step with fear and trembling. Only the Lord Jesus can sustain us in the balance so that we may not topple in to the right, or escaping that, fall to the left. We are surer than ever that God means for us to stand by the cross at the Crossroads to point sinners to the narrow, little-traveled road that starts at the cross and leads by it on up to heaven and the life the Lord has prepared for them who love Him. How can any be saved without this salvation? How can any escape who neglect this salvation?

> *For if the word spoken by angels was steadfast, and every transgression and disobedience received a just recompense of reward; how shall we escape, if we neglect so great salvation?*
> (Hebrews 2:2–3)

eight

The End of This Age and the Return of Christ

Chapter 8

The End of This Age and the Return of Christ

D uring this mighty outpouring of the Holy Spirit, by vision and prophecy we were repeatedly warned that the end of the present age and the return of our Lord are at hand. The Holy Spirit made this great climax at the consummation of this present age so vivid and real that no doubt was left in any of our minds that the Lord God was bringing final and supremely important messages to His people.

The Scriptures teach that the present age will end in the greatest tribulation the world has ever seen and that immediately after that tribulation the Lord will return to destroy the wicked and reward the righteous (Matthew 24:29–30).

The Scriptures also teach that this age will reach its climax at the harvest when the tares will have reached full fruition and when the wheat has passed from the leaf and the blade to the full grain in the ear. When both the wheat and the tares are ripe, the angels will come with the Lord to gather the harvest and to separate the wheat from the tares. (See Mark 4:26–32.) In other words, when the Kingdom of the devil is at its worst and the Kingdom of God on earth is at its best, in its purest form—the evil ripe and the good ripe—then will come the harvest. The Bible further teaches that evil will reach its climax in the incarnation of the devil in control of a demon-deceived, tormented world and that this devil-possessed world ruler, this super-man, will be destroyed by the Lord at His coming.

There may be those who take exception to these remarks, but, without detailed discussion of these matters, I will relate, as best I can, the visions and revelations given the Adullam children, who knew little or nothing of the theology involved.

Visions of the End Times

Time after time they spoke in prophecy, saying that a time of famine, pestilence, war, and desolation is coming and that it will be attended with persecution of the people of God, whom He will especially equip and protect in this crisis.

One boy saw a vision of a Christian trying to buy a measure of rice. So great a crowd surrounded the granary that the Christian could only hope for success in making his purchase by pushing with the crowd. Each man could buy only one measure of rice.[1]

In another vision, one ignorant, uneducated boy was transported to other lands and saw the people getting ready for war, making bombs, and implements of destruction.

The coming of the devil and his incarnation in the Antichrist was prophesied many times, as well as seen in visions.

The children saw a dragon, the devil with seven heads. One boy saw angels fighting with him and seven of his angels. The devil and his angels were overcome and flung out of heaven to earth. (See Revelation 12.)

---

[1] Note: According to certain Bible teachings, the second coming of Jesus will be accomplished in two phases: the *"caught up"* church (1 Thessalonians 4:15–17), followed by the great tribulation which will end when Jesus returns to the earth to establish His kingdom. (See Revelation 19:11–16.) If this is so, the Addulam visions of Christians being persecuted during the tribulation might have to do with converts after the rapture. (See Revelation 7:9–14.)

Adullam boys saw the super-man the world is wishing for, the greatest subject of worship that Buddhism, Theosophy, Islam, and other religions expect. In him, they saw the devil incarnated as a handsome, strong man in the beauty and strength of young manhood.

They also had visions of the image that this God-defying Antichrist will erect according to prophesy as an object of worship, the image that will be able to speak and to deceive the world. (See 2 Thessalonians 2:4.) I asked them how they knew this handsome man of power was the Antichrist. They said that a host of demons followed him everywhere, obeyed his every command, advanced at his word, and halted at his order.

They spoke in prophecy, saying that a time of famine, pestilence, war, and desolation is coming.

This Antichrist was also seen upon a plain as a beast with seven heads. (See Revelation 13:1.) Again I asked how they knew this was the Antichrist, and the children said the angels told them. I have already explained that, as with John, these revelations were given through angels when the children were *"in the Spirit"* and that, like him, they carried on conversation with the angels and by these heavenly messengers were told the mystery of many things they did not understand themselves.

During the reign of this super-man in his God-defying power, the saints of God were standing true and bearing faithful testimony in spite of every hardship and every danger. They saw the two witnesses in Jerusalem (see Revelation 11:3–13), and they saw the saints, as well as these two, endued with mighty supernatural power to fight with and to resist the power of darkness in that awful time, the like of which has never been upon the earth—the time when the devil and all his angels and demons will be turned loose upon the earth, having great wrath, knowing their time is short.

During this time, when no one but a true Spirit-filled saint could stand for a day against such satanic power and supernatural manifestations, the children saw the saints filled with even greater supernatural power of their God, the Spirit of Him who is greater than *"he that is in the world."* They had visions of preaching the gospel in the midst of great persecution; they were given such power that by a word from them, enemies were smitten by plagues or death. This power seemed to issue from within and came out of their mouths;

with it they rebuked and slew their enemies. They were exercising the power the Lord had promised his disciples, power to do the works He did and greater works. (See John 14:12.)

In some visions, after giving testimony in a town that rejected them and having left it at a distance, fire from heaven descended and destroyed the wicked place, even as Sodom and Gomorrah were swept away. When persecution was bitter, they were sometimes caught away bodily by the Holy Spirit as was Philip and as the prophets supposed Elijah had been. (See 2 Kings 2:16.) They were carried away by the Spirit to a place of safety. In time of hunger and need, food was miraculously provided—manna, fruit, and other food. Angels ministered to them. Strength and boldness were given to bear a fearless testimony.

The Christians had power to speak with tongues in the languages of strange and heathen tribes. When, in visions, the boys and girls were thus preaching in the Spirit, we ourselves could see how this might be true, for while one speaker preached to the people of a strange language whom he saw before him, another interpreted for him. (See 1 Corinthians 14:28.) Both spoke in other tongues. One spoke a few sentences, then the other interpreted.

John saw an angel flying in heaven with the everlasting gospel to be preached to all tribes and tongues, just before the fall of Babylon the Great. (See Revelation 14:6–7.) He also saw the great multitude no man could number, people of every tribe and language, who had washed their robes in the blood of the Lamb and had come out of great Tribulation. Just as the Scriptures have prophesied and as the children saw in visions, the gospel will be preached again under angelic ministration in the miraculous power of the Holy Spirit

The gospel will again be preached in the miraculous power of the Holy Spirit.

in a supernatural way, far exceeding that of the early church in the days of its persecution. Could it not be that the harvest outpouring of the Holy Spirit, the latter rain, will far exceed the seed-time outpouring of the Holy Spirit, the former rain, the outpouring on the day of Pentecost?

In those days of the most perfect and supernatural church the world has ever seen, and in the midst of the greatest persecution by the greatest concentration of satanic demonical power and devil-controlled human power that any age on earth has ever experienced, the Adullam children saw the Antichrist, the super-man world leader, marshalling his forces for the final world war of the age.

They also saw the war in the spirit realm. In this they saw a man on a white horse, leading his army dressed in white. They also saw a rider on a red horse, the rider dressed in beautiful dark colored array and followed by his host of demons in black. (See Revelation 6.)

Some visions of the war on earth were also seen. Children saw battleships destroyed by bombs thrown from airplanes, and they saw the ships enter their watery grave to be seen no more. Armies were seen gathered from all the earth, engaged in the great and terrible struggle. The children watched the awful battle. Poison gas and deadly instruments of war destroyed their victims in countless numbers. At first the dead were buried, but later the number of dead were so many they were piled in heaps or left to decay as manure upon the face of the earth, as the prophet has foretold. (See Jeremiah 25:31–33.)

The Return of Christ

In the midst of all this chaos, everything was interrupted by the sudden return of Christ. The sun became dark and the moon red like blood. The stars fell in showers. The heavens shook and seemed to roll together as a scroll. There was a great earthquake that rent the earth asunder. Great crevices opened and people were swallowed alive. Buildings were shaken down, collapsing like children's toy houses, killing and burying the tenants.

While these things in heaven and earth were taking place, the Lord appeared in the heavens. Old and young, rich and poor were overcome with deadly fear. They fled in every direction in wild confusion. Men fled from their shops empty handed, without a thought of their valuables that a few moments earlier had seemed of great importance. Families rushed from their homes without even a glance back upon the luxuries that had been their passion. In one moment, all men became one in purpose; they had only one desire; they sought only one thing—to flee from the face of the returning Judge; they sought only a place of refuge to hide from the visible King of Kings. Some who were not killed by falling houses or who did not tumble into the opened earth tried to flee to the mountains for safety; some leaped into rivers and perished; some turned their own weapons upon themselves.

Everywhere was wailing and shrieking. Everywhere was riot and terror. Anything to escape from the wrath of the Lamb, for the great day of His wrath had come. After this there were visions of the great supper of God, where the beasts and birds were bidden to eat the unburied dead that lay scattered over the ruined earth. Dogs and wild animals were seen feeding on the carcasses of men. Birds and scavengers of the air joined in this supper prepared by God.

In the midst of all this chaos, everything was interrupted by the sudden return of Christ.

While the boys were witnessing this great feast, we could hear their remarks and see their movements as the scene was described and acted out before us.

One would say, "Look at that eagle eating that rich fellow. See it picking his fancy clothes from his body? Look at that! It has taken a piece of his flesh and flown away."

Another said, "Oh, look over there; a vulture and a crow both eating at that man. The vulture has the most courage. He just picks away, gorging himself, never taking time to look up, but the crow is afraid; he takes a bit and looks around to see if he is in danger. Do you see that? Look at the birds standing on that well dressed fellow and digging into him."

Then the boys suddenly wheeled away from the repellent scene, while their remarks, as well as their motions, made it clear enough the sort of abhorring scenes that will characterize the final feast of the earth. Here will be the rich and mighty, the rulers of the earth, the owners of industry, the holders of wealth, the commanding officers of war, and the leaders of all Christ-rejecting enterprises and religions. They will not be there as honored guests, but as the food for the scavengers of the earth over which they have lived in selfish luxury.

The Adullam children witnessed first-hand the terrible culminating scenes of our boasted material civilization. They saw the fruit of godless living and the answer to the question of our Lord, *"For what is a man profited, if he shall gain the whole world, and lose his own soul?"* (Matthew 16:26). The Word of God tells us that all of the nations that forget God are destined to be cast into hell. (See Psalm 9:17.) These simple children believe without a doubt, because they have been shown by God and the angels what is also written in the Word of the Lord, that the climax and consummation of the present world with its human systems of education and its boasted organization and wealth will be "the great supper of God," where the flesh of the dead will be more of a prize than will be the splendor and culture that is now the pride of the living.

Finally, the children saw the Lord and his angels bind the Antichrist hand and foot, preparatory to casting him alive into hell. (See Revelation 19:20.)

There were also visions of the devil taken alive to the mouth of the pit; a box-like lid was lifted up, and he was cast down into the black shaft of the abyss; the lid was shut, and the Lord locked it with a great key. (See Revelation 20:1–3.)

We have written of the visions of the return of Christ as related to the wicked. There were equally clear visions relating to the saints. Our Adullam children saw the heavens open and the Lord descend in glory attended by His angels. On both sides and following the Lord was a great army of attendants in white. Those in front blew beautiful trumpets, and with the blast of trumpets the Lord and His army descended in perfect order, every one keeping in his proper place and rank. As the Lord descended toward the earth there were wonderful visions of the resurrection and rapture of the saints. Graves burst open as from an explosion. Bodies came out of the graves and were suddenly clothed by the heavenly tabernacle of the resurrection life. In some cases, bones were seen to come together—as the children expressed it in Chinese idiom: "one bone from the east, one from the west." These were scattered bones, having become clothed with flesh and transformed into the resurrection body, were caught up to meet the Lord in the air. One boy saw a funeral procession where a Christian was being carried to his burial. On the way to the burial ground, the trumpet sounded, the Lord descended, the coffin opened, the dead man sat up, arose transformed, and ascended into the air.

> The children of Adullam saw the saints enjoying the fellowship of Christ and the angels.

I have already told of how our children had visions of some of our Adullam children who had previously died and now were in heaven, clothed in white and enjoying paradise. And of their seeing the saints of old clothed in white. The Scripture teaches that between death and the resurrection the saints have spiritual bodies and that the saints are clothed in white before the time of the resurrection. (See Revelation 6:9–11.) When I cross-examined the children as to how they knew whether the saints they saw in heaven had been resurrected or not, they said they did not know until the angels told them that they saw only the souls of the saints and that their bodies had not been resurrected. I questioned and re-questioned in some of these matters, yet always received a uniform testimony: the children always saw the saints in white; the saints never had wings; all of the angels had wings; there was no difficulty in distinguishing between saints and angels.

The Wedding Feast

In summary, then, the children of Adullam saw the saints in white now in heaven, with access to paradise, and enjoying the fellowship of Christ and the angels. They saw the descent of the Lord with *"all the holy ones"*—all his angels—at the sounding of the last trumpet. They saw the resurrection and transformation of the bodies of the saints and their ascent into the air.

They also saw the marriage supper of the Lamb. Great tables were spread in paradise in the midst of its magnificent trees, its wonderful flowers with enchanting fragrance, and its glorious birds that sang their carols of praise, where all redeemed animal and vegetable creation was one harmonious, Spirit-filled, God-praising whole. Here, then, in this indescribable paradise of God were spread the tables for the great marriage supper. Angels and the glorified saints skipped about everywhere playing harps, blowing trumpets, singing, and praising the Lord. The children hurried to their jewel bedecked homes to get their harps or trumpets and joined the Spirit-inspired music of the greatest of all festival scenes, the climax of all the hopes of the ages. Great companies sang and danced and praised the King. Others hurried about preparing the tables or the seats and carrying the golden dishes of food.

There was an abundance of food, everything having flavor of its own, exceeding anything that could be imagined.

When all was ready, the call was sent forth and the saints of all past ages gathered around the tables to celebrate the wedding of the King's Great Son. The consummation of all their hopes, the realization of all highest joy in heaven itself, came to its highest point when the harlot, the beggar, the sinner, and the one-time off-scourings of the earth came from the east and the west and sat down with Abraham, Isaac, and Jacob at this festal table in the Kingdom of God. As all arose and expectancy reached its greatest height, the Son Himself came in and sat down at the tables surrounded by his blood-bought and white-robe-clad bride—the redeemed of every nation, and tribe, and tongue— and drank with them the fruit of the vine.

The Final Judgment

The children of Adullam also saw visions of the Day of Judgment. They saw the books in which the deeds of men are recorded and saw the Judge upon the throne before whom all men were judged out of the books. The righteous were set apart to stand in one great company on the one side, while those whose names were not in the book of life were gathered into another great company to stand on the other side. The one company was separated to enter the Kingdom of God and the life of the ages; the other group was doomed to go into the fire prepared for the devil and his angels.

A few were privileged to have visions of the new heaven and earth. The new heaven was so filled with Shekinah glory that the children could not gaze directly into it.

The New Jerusalem, the four-square city, occupied the central position, having descended to the new earth. The whole new earth was much like the paradise in the city. It was the new heaven and the new earth that had passed through the new birth and that will never pass away, the earth where God will again pitch His tent with men, where He will forever be called their God and they shall all and always be His children. Amen.

nine

Chinese Beggar Boy Prophesies

Chapter 9

Chinese Beggar Boy Prophesies

n fulfillment of the Scripture that *"in the last days…your sons… shall prophesy"* (Acts 2:17), one of the little ten-year-old beggar sons of China was used as the direct mouth-piece of the Lord to bring us a message by direct inspiration.

A few months previous, this boy, ragged and dirty—in fact, more nearly clothed with filth than with garments—came to our door with his two companions to ask if he might come in. When bathed and dressed, the boy looked like a guileless little fellow, and such he proved to be. He at once took every Bible story and sermon to heart. Soon, he learned to pray and could be heard praying earnestly in bed every night. When the Holy Spirit fell upon us, this boy was among the first to receive the baptism in the Spirit, speaking with other tongues as on the day of Pentecost.

In the past, God spoke through men who were moved upon by the Holy Spirit, so that Scripture was inspired of God. Prophets declared their message to be *"Thus saith the Lord"* with such assurance that they were ready to back their convictions with their lives. Even today, the living God still reigns and speaks to men by direct prophecy when the circumstances demand it and when faith and other conditions are according to His divine will.

The Littlest Preacher

One night the power of the Lord was present in an unusual manner. Heaven seemed not far away. Then our one-time, little, friendless beggar-boy seemed to leave this filthy earth and to be caught up to heaven. Ushered into the presence of the Lord Jesus, he fell prostrate at His feet in humble adoration and worship. The boy lay there in the middle of the room surrounded by his companions, who sat about him on the floor, listening intently to a message that came through him from the Lord. Such gripping, heart-searching words I have never heard.

While the boy sobbed and wept with deepest grief, the message was given a sentence or two at a time in a clear strong voice. The language came in rhythm; the words were simple and pure. The intonation of voice, the choice of language, the penetrating power of every word was such that no person who heard could ever doubt that this little simple-minded Samuel was speaking by direct supernatural inspiration from God.

Prostrated in vision at the feet of the Lord, the boy said, "Lord Jesus, I am not worthy to be here or to be saved at all. I am only a little street beggar."

Then Jesus addressed the boy. The boy did not know it at the time, but the Lord actually spoke through the boy as a mouthpiece, using the first person while addressing the crowd gathered about him.

No one doubted that Samuel was speaking by direct supernatural inspiration from God.

This message was given between heartrending sobs and floods of tears from the boy. Here is the *"Thus saith the Lord"* that we wish might grip your hearts as it still grips our own:

I weep tonight. I am heartbroken. I am in deep sorrow because those who believe in me are so very few. I planned and pre-pared heaven for everyone, having made room for all the people in all the world. I made the New Jerusalem in three great cities, one above the other, with plenty of space for all men. But men will not believe me. Those who believe are so very few. I am sad, so very sad. Since men will not believe me, I must destroy the wicked earth. I planned to visit it with three great calamities, but it is so wicked that I have added a fourth.

If you have any friends, tell them to repent quickly; persuade all men as rapidly as possible to believe in the gospel; but if the people will not listen and will not accept your message, the responsibility will not be upon you.

Receive the baptism of the Holy Spirit. If you will tarry and believe, I will baptize you. The devil deceives you by making you think you will not receive the baptism, but wait and seek and I will baptize you, and give you power to cast out devils and to heal the sick. Those who receive the seal of the Holy Spirit are to preach and testify, and I will be with you to help and protect you in times of danger.

If you think perhaps you will not get to heaven, that thought is of the devil. I will not destroy my own children; I will protect and save every one; not one of mine will perish. I will overcome. Pray for Mr. and Mrs. Baker and I will give them power to cast out devils and heal the sick. The children in the home should obey. Do not fight. Do not lie. Live at peace. When you pray, pray from the heart. Do not let your love grow cold.

Tell other churches they, too, should seek the Holy Spirit. ALL CHURCHES MUST PRESS FORWARD.

The devil is coming to earth in a few years, and there will be great tribulation. Do not worry; I will protect and care for you.

People everywhere will gather together and fight in one place, after which I will come to punish the earth. You must not fear, for those who believe in me will be caught up to blow trumpets and to play harps.

I will destroy two of every three. When I come everything must obey my voice. Houses will tumble down; mountains will fall; trees will be destroyed. There will be utter destruction where I will not leave on blade of grass. Those who worship idols will perish. All sorcerers and mediums shall be cast into hell. Only those who believe the gospel will be saved.

This is the message that the Lord gave to Adullam and, we believe, to all those who will hear our testimony of this prophesy. This word from our risen Lord was delivered to us in Chinese, the sentences spoken slowly and distinctly with pauses between phrases. I wrote them down immediately as they were given, and I often repeated them a time or two so there could be no mistake on the part of the hearers. There was ample time to record without out mistake every word the Lord spoke through this little inspired prophet of His choice.

> The boy arose and told us he had been at the feet of Jesus.

With his message complete, the boy arose and told us he had been at the feet of Jesus. He did not know that the Lord had spoken through him as well as to him in the first person. He repeated the prophecy, saying, "Jesus said that, Jesus said this," etc.

Thus Saith the Lord

The fact that this prophecy was heard, written out, and then repeated from the little prophet's memory, item by item, made it easy to envision how in days of old the prophets spoke as moved by God, how a scribe might record every word as it came from the lips of the prophet, or how the prophet himself could record his own messages, truly saying, *"Thus saith the Lord."*

In day of old, when religious and worldly men had departed from a simple faith in a personal living God who spoke to men and when their unbelief and wickedness was such that *"in those days; there was no open vision"* (1 Samuel 3:1), God found a pure-minded little Samuel and, in an audible voice, spoke to him a message that was fulfilled to the very letter. Accordingly, we believe that God, who is still the same living God that has spoken to and through others in the past, has given to us through our little Chinese Samuel a *"Thus saith the Lord"* that will shortly come to pass, a message to be heeded to our eternal joy or neglected to our eternal sorrow.

ten

Some Light on
Writing the Bible

Chapter 10

Some Light on Writing the Bible

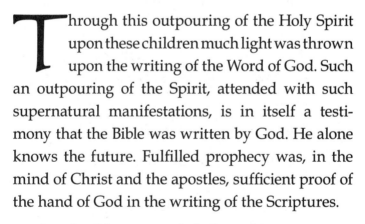

Through this outpouring of the Holy Spirit upon these children much light was thrown upon the writing of the Word of God. Such an outpouring of the Spirit, attended with such supernatural manifestations, is in itself a testimony that the Bible was written by God. He alone knows the future. Fulfilled prophecy was, in the mind of Christ and the apostles, sufficient proof of the hand of God in the writing of the Scriptures.

In what I have recorded about this outpouring of the Holy Spirit upon these children, ten prophecies of the Scriptures were fulfilled:

1. Such a baptism was prophesied for believers of the present age (see Joel 2:28–29).

2. It was to be accompanied by speaking in unknown languages (see 1 Corinthians 14:21).

3. It was to be accompanied by prophesying as the Spirit gave utterance (see Acts 2:17).

4. These children were shown *"the things of Christ"* (John 16:14).

5. The reality of *"things to come"* (John 16:13) was shown them.

6. They were born again of the Holy Spirit, receiving the witness in their hearts, *"crying, 'Abba Father'"* (Galatians 4:6).

7. The written Word was fulfilled that in the last days *"young men shall see visions"* (Acts 2:17).

8. Demons were cast out. (See Mark 16:17.)

9. The sick were miraculously healed, just as the Bible said they might be, by the power of the Holy Spirit (see Mark 16:18).

10. A miraculous change took place so that things once loved were hated and things once hated were loved. (See 2 Corinthians 5:17.)

It is to be recalled that, according to the Bible, the revelations of God and the writings of the

Scriptures are independent of natural ability or of acquired education. Uneducated men such as Amos, Peter, and John, inspired by God, wrote more profoundly than the wisest of this world.

God Still Speaks

In what the Lord has done and revealed to these despised and outcast beggar boys and girls, can we not see a proof of the Word of God? While *"not many wise men after the flesh, not many mighty"* follow the old-fashioned, narrow way of simple faith in God, He still can and does choose these *"which are despised"* (1 Corinthians 1:28), even these simple Chinese children of the streets and gutters, to *"bring to naught things that are"* (1 Corinthians 1:28).

While the wise of this educated, proud, and stiff-necked generation go on groping around in the darkness of their own self-sufficient delusions, it must be true in this day, as in the past, that in the midst of so much confusion of man's wisdom, Jesus can still say, *"I thank Thee, O Father, Lord of heaven* and earth, because thou hast hid these things from the wise and prudent, and hast revealed them unto babes" (Matthew 11:25).

As a whole, the educated and the rulers of the days of Christ did not understand His miraculous works and life, or *"they would not have crucified the Lord of glory"* (1 Corinthians 2:8). The rulers and the educated of the days of the apostles did not understand the miraculous working of Almighty God through simple men endued with the power of the Holy Spirit, or they would not have killed the Spirit-filled saints of the early church. The profound revelations to these Chinese children, not having been educated in the institutions of higher learning, is corroboration that the written Word of God came through openhearted men independent of natural ability or acquired education.

Divine Inspiration

Some clear light was thrown on the way Bible writers might have had eyewitness knowledge of events already passed. One of our naturally most ignorant and untalented boys was, on more than one occasion, when "in the Spirit" an eyewitness of the principal historical events of the Old and New Testaments. He saw the plagues of Egypt: the frogs in the King's palace, the flies in Pharaoh's food, the locusts, the eldest son dead with the whole family in consternation. He also saw Elijah and Elisha cross the Jordan, the chariots of fire, and Elijah's ascension. Daniel was seen in the lion's den with his angel guard, and other Old Testament events were likewise seen.

This boy was also given visions of the miracles of Christ. He saw the temptations of the Lord. He watched as the devil, in the form of a handsome young man, led the Lord to a high mountain and in vision showed Him the kingdoms of the world. Angels followed Jesus wherever He went. There were visions of Christ walking on the water, healing the sick, and opening the eyes of the blind. This boy and others saw the passion of the Lord Jesus, His resurrection, and His ascension.

At first I wondered at these visions of past events. I then remembered that with God there is no past, present, or future. He is the Great I Am. All things are like the present with Him. Since the Holy Spirit is His Spirit, by visions and revelations of the Spirit, past, present, and future may, in God's economy, be made "present" to any individual to whom the Lord chooses to make such revelations.

These revelations of the past to the children of Adullam corroborate the inspiration of the Bible.

It was easy for God to take Moses and others, by vision, through past events or future events just as an eyewitness will sees present events. It was easy for these biblical giants to be able to record the past, the present, and the future in the one and only Book that records the end from the beginning and the beginning from the end.

The Holy Spirit showed us by illustration how some parts of the Bible became divine records of supernatural revelations. When the children were "in the Spirit," describing scenes they were seeing in visions, the Spirit caused one boy, who was also in a trance, lost "in the Spirit," to sit down and go through the motions of writing item by item what the others were seeing and describing. Thus anyone should be able to see how easy it was for God to write a Bible. One could record what another saw and described.

> These revelations of the past to the children of Adullam corroborate the inspiration of the Bible.

If God can now take an ignorant, illiterate beggar boy from a dirty Chinese street, or a half-wild tribes-boy from a remote mountain solitude, and fill him with the Holy Spirit, while allowing him to see as an eye witness the things beyond the veil—things of the present, things of the past, things to come—has it not always been just as easy for God to reveal everything that is written in the Bible to any vessel of His choosing and have a Baruch sit by his side to write just what was seen and revealed, recording word for word any and every prophecy just as it came from the Lord God? (See Jeremiah 36:4.)

If our boys can be caught into the presence of the Lord and come back saying, "The Lord said," couldn't prophets of old record their own prophecy or visions and say with absolute truth, *"Thus saith the Lord?"*

How God, with whom past, present, and future is all the same, can reveal past, present, and future events as present events, I do not know. The Bible says he can. The Bible says He did. The people of Adullam know He still does.

If men ever spoke in prophecy as they were moved by the Holy Spirit, if men were ever *"in the Spirit on the Lord's Day"* (Revelation 1:10) and caught up to heaven, if men were given visions *"in the year King Uzziah died"* (Isaiah 6:10), then they can still be moved upon by the Holy Spirit and prophesy. They can still be caught away *"in the Spirit"* and see the unseen worlds beyond the veil. They can still see such visions any number of years after King Uzziah died.

The same God is still on the same throne, reigning over the same world, dealing with the same world, dealing with the same kind of evil hearts, through the same sort of men, with the same kind of dispositions and passions Elijah had.

Since God does, now in this day, reveal Himself through prophecy, vision, and revelations—as He is revealing himself all around the world—He has, therefore, revealed Himself just as the Bible said He did in the days of old to the prophets and saints.

In this wicked age, in the midst of this present unbelieving, perverse generation, the Lord can and will prove that what He has written in the Bible is the Word of the living God. He can and does move in the midst of a believing people in supernatural ways through gifts of the Holy Spirit, confirming the Word with signs following. (See Mark 16:15-30.)

eleven

The Homeland

Chapter 11

The Homeland

I n view of what we have written, it is clear enough that the Lord has used every means that is necessary to assure us that in the Bible we have *"a more sure word of prophecy"* (2 Peter 1:19) to which we should take heed.

It has also been made clear enough that the great purpose of that former word of prophesy and the present day visions and prophecy in our midst is so we may know as a certainty that there is a wonderful homeland just beyond the veil. No "stranger," no "pilgrim" is ever satisfied. The satisfying portion is still ahead at the end of the journey.

It may be that as the journey leads over difficult pathways and exhausting mountains, the pilgrim may become so wearied with his heavy burdens that he can scarcely hear the singing of the birds, sense refreshment from the wayside flowers, or find any great happiness in the fellowship of his fellow pilgrims. But it will not be so at the end of the way.

Our Eternal Reward

The stooped and wearied bodies of life's pilgrims will be renewed when they reach their eternal homeland. *"We shall all be changed, in a moment, in the twinkling of an eye....For this corruptible must put on incorruption"* (1 Corinthians 15:51–53). Old age will vanish. There will be no old men in heaven, no faltering steps of the aged. No faded sight, no deafened hearing, no crippled body encumbers any of the people in the whole of that bright city.

There is a city that never gets dark, nor does it need the sun by day or the moon by night. Its golden streets require no sweeping. Its jewel-bedecked dwellings need no repair. There is a city that has no doctor's offices, no diseased and disabled, no sickness or sorrow; a city with no crepe on its golden doors, no funeral processions on its golden streets; a city where melancholy and all mourning is done away; a city where all death has been swallowed up by life and that more abundantly; a city of pure unbounded joy.

There is a land of unclouded day where storm clouds never rise. In that happy land there is no unemployment or struggle for survival. There is no selfish competition. There is no self-seeking to engender unloving suspicion. No one is anxious as to what he shall eat or what he shall wear. The garments of white will never grow threadbare. The trees with the fruits of life will never be barren.

The water of life will never run dry, and whosoever desires may drink. All the joy and enthusiasm of the most jubilant youth is the inheritance of every soul in heaven. We are not unthankful for days of happiness here on earth. But in our most happy moments we are still only a vessel of clay. Even in our highest moments, we sense a still greater joy, a happiness almost within reach of our hands, but before it can be grasped we are dragged away by the weight of the clay.

> All the joy and enthusiasm of the most jubilant youth is the inheritance of every soul in heaven.

Here on earth, children frolic and play. They run, and roll, and they leap for joy. They sing and they shout. At times their joy and happiness seem complete. *"Of such is the kingdom of heaven"* (Matthew 19:14). But the highest exuberant joys and the most ecstatic thrills of bliss on earth cannot compare to the greater *"joy unspeakable"* (1 Peter 1:8) when this body of hindering clay has been replaced by the body that is real.

In the New Jerusalem everybody is in love with everybody else. Being "in love" on earth is nothing compared with being "in love" in the land of glory. Not a flaw, not an imperfection, not an unlovely trait will detract from being perfectly and altogether "in love" with everybody.

The Music of Heaven

The kingdom of heaven is a land of music. When God made man He put music in his soul. But the discords of the mud have spoiled the harmony. The lost chord will never be found until it is found in heaven when we are clothed upon with the tabernacle that is from above. The finest, the sweetest, the most perfect music on earth is but a seeking for the lost chords and harmonies the redeemed and the angels sing in heaven. The finest instruments of music that have been made on earth, from the days when the descendants of Adam began to *"handle the harp and organ"* (Genesis 4:21) until the present day, are but mere imitations of the trumpets, harps, and instruments upon which "the lost chords" are restored in the golden city and upon which all the music of the liberated soul can find its fullest expression.

Much of the music and the rhythm the Father placed in the souls of His children have since been turned by the devil into evil channels for pleasure and the lust of the perverted flesh. From the wildest barbarians on remote islands to the pleasure intoxicated revelers of the fashionable clubs, men and women dance in musical rhythm in pursuit of sensual pleasure. In heaven, to the tune of music that is holy and pure, the redeemed join the angels dancing in "joy" that is beyond all earthly or natural "pleasure" in the rhythm to which the stars are swinging and singing in their orbits.

> On earth we see little—and understand less—of the beauties of God's creation.

There is a park in the city, an Eden park of pleasure and fruit. Here, where the unreal has been replaced by the real, in all God's animal and plant creation there is nothing that hurts or destroys in the entire holy mount.

On earth we see little—and understand less—of the beauties of God's creation. The dirt and the dust of the earth have clouded the windows of our soul. We scarcely see through the glass even darkly. When God has brushed away the encumbrances and opened the eyes of the soul, for the first time will we really look upon and appreciate the glories of God's wonderful creation.

There is a park where birds of all plumage are ever singing; there is a land where every ear will be turned to hear soul-stirring anthems; there is a land where flowers of every hue are forever blooming; there is a land where every eye will be opened to see them in their beauty; there is a land where the fragrance of the rose of Sharon and the lily of the valley mingle with a thousand perfumes that man has never known.

Sometimes we seem to see the light of the city beyond the sky, but our vision is lost in the blur of imperfect sight. Sometimes we seem to hear the enchanting music of a different sphere, but the strain is lost in the discord of sounds that are nearer. Sometimes we seem to sense an upward pull away from all that is enslaving, but the attraction of earth holds our feet like fetters. Sometimes the soul would fly to "the land that is fairer than day," but it falls back in disappointment because of its broken wings. He who declares his freedom to walk alone to the city of freedom finds his pathway hopelessly blocked by the things of this world, the flesh, and the devil with no power in himself to overcome.

But there is a way.

twelve

The Way

Chapter 12

The Way

There is only one way. Christ is the way. *"No man cometh unto the Father, but by me"* (John 14:6).

Man is not the way; man can never make a way, nor does man ever know the way to the golden city. The city and the way to the city are both revelations from above.

Christ, who is the way, is not from below. He is from above. It is *"he that came down from heaven, even the Son of man which is in heaven,"* who is *"the great God and our Savior Jesus Christ"* (John 3:13; Titus 2:13).

The natural man does not travel toward the happy city of pure delight. He travels away from it. The longer he walks, the father he gets away from this heavenly city.

Little children belong to the Kingdom of God. They play and frolic at the gates of the city. But when they begin to walk in sin, they always walk away from the city, away from this happy Eden home. The farther they wander and the more they reason—whether they walk alone or follow the crowd—the farther they get from the city, until its light is dimly seen or lost forever. The only way to reach the city is to turn back. *"Except ye be converted, and become as little children, ye shall not enter into the kingdom of heaven"* (Matthew 18:3). But the farther man walks alone, the older he gets, the more he studies with his natural mind, the more he passes turnstiles in his self-conceited course until at last he finds no way of returning to a heart like *"a little child"* (Mark 10:15).

Amazing Grace

"The world by wisdom knew not God" (1 Corinthians 1:21). Man will never find God through study. The man who trusts the workings of his own mind or the minds of other men will never see the city of God.

Man, on the merits of his character, will never walk the golden streets. What a man is, what a man does, or how a man lives has nothing to do with his salvation. On the basis of how "good" he is, the best man on earth has no more hope of heaven than the worst man on earth. Man who trusts in his own character, his own moral goodness, is only a modern Pharisee with eyes blinded to the truth. The publican, the drunkard, the harlot, depending and trusting in Jesus, will enter the city of God, while that "good" man will be cast into outer darkness where *"there shall be weeping and gnashing of teeth"* (Matthew 8:12).

"By grace are ye saved… not of works" (Ephesians 2:8–9). Salvation is something God gives. It is not something man is or is not. Salvation is from above. It is not from below, or from within, or from among men.

> Jesus came from heaven to save sinners, not righteous people with good character.

That which is born from below is flesh and born by the will of man. Those born from below, no matter how wise or good or bad they may become, must be born again from above. They become the children of God *"which were born, not of blood, nor of the will of the flesh, nor of the will of man, but of God…. Except a man be born again, he cannot see the kingdom of God"* (John 1:13; 3:3). This birth, that every accountable man must have who will ever see God or sing the songs of the redeemed in the city beyond the sky, is a supernatural birth. It is altogether from above. Joining a church, singing hymns, reading or saying prayers, working in or for the church, preaching from the pulpit, or giving all one's body to be burned has nothing whatever to do with the new birth. The new birth is something that God gives by grace regardless of works.

Unless Ye Be Born Again

The finest pulpit orator, the most formal churchman, the most protesting protestant has no more hope of heaven than the most reckless sinner, unless he be born again.

The Lord was so anxious to have me return that He made the way simple and plain. I was a sinner living selfishly and not for the glory of God. I had turned to my own way. *"All have sinned, and come short of the glory of God....There is none righteous, no, not one....They are all gone out of the way"* (Romans 3:23; 3:10; 3:12). I was among that number.

Jesus came from heaven to save sinners, not righteous people with good character. Thus I had my chance. I should have suffered the penalty of my sin, but Christ loved me and died in my stead. He bore my *"sins in His own body on the tree"* (1 Peter 2:24). Christ died on the cross—the Sinless One instead of the sinner. He *"who knew no sin"* (2 Corinthians 5:21) died in my place on the cross where I should have died. I, the sinning Barabbas, the punishment-deserving sinner, was set absolutely and unconditionally free. *"He hath made Him to be sin for us, who knew no sin: that we might be made the righteousness of God in Him"* (verse 21). God punished Jesus, so He will not punish me. Because He forsook Jesus, He will not forsake me. All I

> I, the punishment-deserving sinner, was set absolutely and unconditionally free.

had to be was to be a sinner. All I had to do was to do nothing.

I simply believed that Jesus did it all.

He that believeth on me hath everlasting life.
(John 6:47)

He that heareth My word, and believeth on Him that sent me, hath everlasting life, and shall not come into condemnation; but is passed from death unto life. (John 5:24)

As many as received Him, to them gave He power to become the sons of God, even to them that believe on His name. (John 1:12)

Having believed that Jesus did what He said He did, and having accepted Him as my substitute and as my sin-bearer, He accepted me as His child. He sent His Holy Spirit into my heart, so that I was born from above. The Holy Spirit in my heart bore witness crying, *"Abba, Father."*

Before that, I had worked. Now God worked in me to will and do His good will. The things I once loved I now hated, and the things I once hated I now loved. Now the more I try to be good the worse it goes. The more I believe God works in me and for me the better it goes.

The Lord has shown me the light of the city ahead.

> *I know whom I have believed, and am persuaded that He is able to keep that which I have committed unto Him against that day.*
>
> (2 Timothy 1:12)

I shall surely enter by the gates into the city to share the joys of those who overcome by simple faith because of the blood of the Lamb.

Jesus finished our salvation. He died for the sins of the whole world. Eternal life is a "gift." *"The gift of God is eternal life through Jesus Christ our Lord"* (Romans 6:23). This gift is free. All we have to do is accept it or reject it, take it or ignore it. We must be like one of the two thieves crucified to Jesus' left and right: either believe that Jesus is God and can save a sinner who acknowledges his condition, and spend eternity with Christ in paradise; or, be like the other thief and refuse to believe that Jesus is God, and die in our unforgiven sins away from God.

Jesus saves any and all on the basis of faith. *"Whosoever believeth in Him should not perish, but have everlasting life"* (John 3:16). Those who believe and are thus saved, Jesus keeps. They don't hold the Rock; the Rock holds them. They do not hold Jesus; Jesus holds them. They are saved by grace through faith apart from works.

> *This is the victory that overcometh the world, even our faith. Who is he that overcometh the world, but he that believeth that Jesus is the Son of God?* (1 John 4:4–5)

Those who are saved by grace and kept by grace live lives of repentance, do the works of righteousness, and perform religious duties because they are saved already, not in order to be saved. The work they do is because of what God has put in them from above.

The saved have become *"partakers of the divine nature"* (2 Peter 1:4). *"If any man have not the Spirit of*

Christ, he is none of His" (Romans 8:9). All of Christ's children have the Holy Spirit in their bodies and hearts and have been born again. *"I am crucified with Christ: nevertheless I live; yet not I, but Christ liveth in me"* (Galatians 2:20). Christ within caused all my works that please him, *"for it is God which worketh in you both to will and do of His good pleasure"* (Philippians 2:13).

The saved are heavenly citizens who love not the world, nor the things of the world. They have as much of the "heaven life" now as they have of the Holy Spirit. The Holy Spirit is the heaven life, the life of God, the eternal life. We have the "earnest," or down payment, on heaven.

Through the deeper experiences of the Holy Spirit, heaven may become more real than earth, so that the child of God may, at times, almost walk by sight as well as by faith on his pilgrim journey to the city whose builder and maker is God.

Our Testimony

Our Adullam message is now complete. This testimony is sent forth, not because of any natural superior knowledge, but because these are things that have happened among us as *"God hath revealed them unto us by His Spirit"* (1 Corinthians 2:10).

There are limitations as to what I can put into writing. Some things can only be known directly through the revelation of the Holy Spirit to one's self. I would like to write more, but I cannot. But what has been written, I have written that you may believe and *"that believing ye might have life through His name"* (John 20:31). Or, having life, that you may be encouraged to press onward until you receive more and more of the abundant life, the life through the baptism and fullness of the Holy Spirit, the life the Lord has planned for each of His children, the foretaste of the Great City of the King, the city of God where all things are made new.

About the Author,
H.A.Baker

About the Author, H. A. Baker

Rev. H. A. Baker and his wife, Josephine, were missionaries to Tibet from 1911 to 1919 before returning to their home in America for several years, believing their missionary days were over due to sickness. But God soon called them to China, to the southwest corner of the Yunnan province. There they settled in a little town called Kotchiu that was home to brigand robbers and said to be the worst town in all of China. In the midst of sinful surroundings, the Bakers let God's light shine out.

The Bakers soon became conscious of the many beggar boys who were starving and dying in the streets. They decided to open the Adullam Home, providing a shelter for these poor homeless children. There were forty boys in the home when a great miracle took place and God poured out His Holy Spirit, revealing the secrets of heaven, hell, and spiritual beings to the orphans. H. A. Baker wrote of these events in his classic book, *Visions Beyond the Veil*.

Heaven Awaits
D. L. Moody

"How can I get to heaven?"

This question is asked by millions of people today. Help, encouragement, and definite answers await the reader, as page after page unfolds with the explanation of this exciting place—heaven—and how we can get there. With tremendous insight, D. L. Moody, a dynamic evangelist who reached thousands of people throughout the world with his special message of Christ's love, offers easy to understand explanations that make this book one that must be read and shared with others.

ISBN: 978-1-60374-036-4 • Pocket • 160 pages

www.whitakerhouse.com

A Place Called Heaven
E. M. Bounds

Christ has gone to prepare a place for you in heaven!
Examining the Scriptures that pertain to heaven, author
E. M. Bounds reveals how you can look forward to receiving
your crown of glory, reigning with Christ forever, and
reuniting with your loved ones. Get a taste of heaven here
on earth, learn a true Christian attitude toward eternity,
and discover how to lay up treasures in your eternal home.
Through Bound's anointed writing, the breathtaking beauty
and joy that await every believer in Christ will become real
to you. You can know that you are heaven-bound!

ISBN: 978-0-88368-958-5 • Trade • 160 pages

www.whitakerhouse.com